Campbell's Rambles

How a Seeing Eye Dog Retrieved My Life

by

Patty L. Fletcher

Patty and Campbell

Copyright 2014 by Patty L. Fletcher

All rights reserved.

ISBN: 1500625884
ISBN-13: 978-1500625887

Legal Notes

THE SEEING EYE® and SEEING EYE® are registered trademarks of The Seeing Eye, Inc.
See: **www.SeeingEye.org**

CONTACT-CONCERN of Northeast Tennessee, Inc.
is a phone help line I&R (Information and Referral) Center
See: **www.CONTACTCONCERN.org**

Table of Contents

Introduction and Thanks 7

Prologue: September 2013 11

Part 1 How Campbell Retrieved My Life 15
    Chapter 1 Preparing for The Seeing Eye 17
    Chapter 2 My Trip and Arrival 23
    Chapter 3 April 4, 2011
        Dog Day: The Most Wonderful Day Ever 29
    Chapter 4 The Connection and That First Walk 33
    Chapter 5 Hell Week 37
    Chapter 6 Learning the Hard Way 43

Part 2 The Home Stretch 49
    Chapter 7 Halfway 51
    Chapter 8 The Mall 59
    Chapter 9 Training 69
    Chapter 10 New York 75
    Chapter 11 Getting the Hang of It 87
    Chapter 12 Last Trip 91
    Chapter 13 Readying Myself To Go Home 97
    Chapter 14 My Last Morning 101

Part 3 The Journey Begins 109
    Chapter 15 False Alarm 111
    Chapter 16 Finally Going Home 119
    Chapter 17 Introducing Campbell to My Life 125
    Chapter 18 Exploring Our New Life Together 131
    Chapter 19 Seeing Summer through New Eyes 139
    Chapter 20 Changing Seasons, Changing Lives 149
    Chapter 21 Yes or No? 159
    Chapter 22 Getting Ready and Keeping Secrets 169
    Chapter 23 Arrival Day 175
    Chapter 24 Like Old Times 189
    Chapter 25 The Route and Visiting 199
    Chapter 26 The Last Day 209

Afterword 221

About the Author
    Patty Lyne Fletcher in Her Own Words — June 2014 227

About Leonore and David Dvorkin 229

Introduction and Thanks

The story you're about to read may make you laugh or cry. Parts of it may anger you. However, I hope most of all that it will leave you with a better understanding of guide dogs and how they're handled, and how the work of learning to handle them affects both the one learning and everyone around that person. I hope that you will come away with a better understanding of blind people and how they work in general, as well as how they work when plagued with other disabilities in addition to their blindness.

First, though, I want to thank a few people for making this whole thing possible—and I do mean the whole thing, from my going to get my Seeing Eye® dog, Campbell, all the way up through the completion of my book. It's possible that I've left someone important off this list. So please know that if you have contributed in some way to my successful life, but you don't see your name below, I'm still very glad to have you in my life.

First, I'd like to thank my friend Phyllis Stevens and her fourth Seeing Eye dog, Emmy. They were the ones who showed me very clearly that yes, I did need a guide dog, and I will be forever grateful to them for that.

Next, I'd like to thank my father. At first, he wasn't sure that my going to get a guide dog was a good idea. Even so, he made sure that I had everything I needed to make my trip to Morristown, New Jersey and The Seeing Eye successful. So thanks, Dad! Campbell says thanks, too. We're really happy together, and we couldn't have gotten together without you. Nor would we still be together today had you not stuck by us through all our successes and trials.

Next is Mr. Drew Gibbon, Sr., Instructor for The Seeing Eye. Right from our very first meeting, Drew made it clear that he was going to be my friend, as well as my instructor. His kind and gentle manner immediately put me at ease, and his tireless work with me from that moment on helped make me who and what I am today. In fact, I'd probably never have written this book had it not been for him. That's because he said to me, over and over, "Come on, young lady! Take a chance. There's a 50 percent chance that you'll be right." So thanks all the way around, Drew. You really did make a huge difference in my life. I hope you'll enjoy the book. I had lots of fun writing it, and as you'll see, you play a major part in it.

Next up is Donnie Starnes. Things didn't turn out for the two of us the way we had planned, but we had some good times, Donnie, and I don't regret our having been together. You helped me rediscover myself. You restored to me the ability to do some things I'd done years before I met you but had lost due to some harsh times in my life. I'll be forever grateful to you, and I have a very special place in my heart for you. May you also eventually know the joy of true freedom, which can only be achieved by being honest with oneself.

Thanks to my daughter, Polly, and my four beautiful grandchildren: Telucia, Katie, Cash, and Jack. You helped me to keep going no matter how hard things got during class at The Seeing Eye. Being able to chat with all of you when I was taking a break helped so much to keep my spirits up. Thanks so much for those snippets of energy.

To my supervisor, Lynn Sorrell, and the entire staff at Contact-Concern of Northeast Tennessee, Inc.: Lynn, you're a wonderful supervisor and friend, and I'm tremendously grateful to you for having adapted so well to my having Campbell. Not all dog handlers are equally fortunate. To the rest of you staff members, including Dawn Fink (now retired): Thanks for being so great with Campbell and for being so understanding of my needs as a blind worker.

(Campbell says, "To heck with all that. Thank Dawn for what's really important, the bed!")

Thanks to the staff and the rest of my training team at The Seeing Eye. You all were and are great. You're always willing to answer questions, and you've never stopped trying to help me improve as a guide dog handler. To recognize a few of you by name: John Keane, David Johnson, Jeff McMullen, and Pauline Alexander. To all of you: Thanks for not giving up on me, for helping me to keep putting one foot in front of the other, even when it was tremendously hard to do that.

To my friend Mike Tate: Your constant support and advice have helped keep me on track, and your honest advice regarding this book has been something I absolutely could not have done without. Now you've written your own book, and I know you hope to have it out sometime in the next few months. Believe me, I'm right there with you all the way!

Finally, thanks to Leonore and David Dvorkin, of Denver, Colorado. Leonore edited this book, and then David did all the additional work necessary for its publication. Without their expertise, patience, and awesome teamwork, I'd never have been able to do this at all. I always wanted to write a book; I always knew I could. I just needed the right tools to help me do it, and when I found the Dvorkins, I found my tools. Thanks for a job well done, Leonore and David.

There is more information about the Dvorkins and their services at the end of the book.

Well, folks, if I've forgotten anyone, just know that I am forever grateful to any of you who stepped up in any way whatsoever to help me along my way.

For now, I wish you happy reading.

May harmony find you, and blessid be.

Patty L. Fletcher

July 2014

(Editor's note: In her writing, the author prefers to spell the words blessed and magic thus: blessid and magik.)

Prologue

September 2013

It's late in the evening here; all is quiet. Campbell is sleeping the peaceful, happy sleep of a satisfied Labrador, dreaming dreams filled with fun at the lake and chasing rabbits, or maybe dreams of leading me along a busy street or across a congested intersection. In either case, he's snuggled up on the foot of Phyllis's bed, sound asleep. It's only fitting that I would sit down here in this house at this time to rewrite the first few pages of my book. After all, it was Phyllis Stevens and her black Lab, Emmy, who led me to go to The Seeing Eye and get Campbell, my first-ever guide dog. It's also just as fitting that we are here this weekend, because Phyllis is going to be leaving tomorrow to go get what will be her fifth guide dog from The Seeing Eye. (Emmy Dog left for the Rainbow Bridge shortly after Phyllis got her new dog.)

And so we begin.

It was a nice spring afternoon in May of 2010. Phyllis, Emmy, and I were out for the day. We'd been shopping and had gone to lunch in the mall. We were returning to the store where Phyllis had left her packages when I made the discovery that yes, I really did need a guide dog.

We had just left one of our favorite places to eat, and not 10 minutes before, I'd asked Phyllis how we would stay together in the mall. She told me to simply listen for the bell on Emmy's collar and to stay right behind her. I was cane traveling at the time and had no idea what was in store for me. Yes, I'd been around plenty of guide dogs and their handlers, but I had had sight then, and I'd never tried to follow a handler in a crowded area—and certainly not while cane traveling totally on my own. So I had no clue what was about to happen to me.

We were going along pretty well, when all of a sudden, we came to a very crowded area in the mall. Emmy found an opening in the crowd, and with Phyllis following along, took it. I was left eating their dust, saying, "Where the hell did they go?" I stood for a moment, letting what had just happened sink in, and then realized that I had not one clue how to get to where Emmy and Phyllis had been going. I'd never walked through this mall—or any mall, for that matter—alone, and so knew nothing of how it was laid out or where to go. So I was forced to ask for and accept help from someone who truly annoyed me. They had this "poor little blind girl" attitude that really gets under my skin.

Once Emmy, Phyllis, and I were back together again and outside waiting for the bus, I asked what had happened. She explained what Emmy had done and apologetically admitted that she hadn't even known we'd been separated until Emmy and she had gotten where they were going. She teased me in a serious sort of way saying, "You know, these things wouldn't happen to you if you didn't spend all day chasing a stick."

I went home that night and gave what she had said some really good thought. The next day, I phoned her to ask how I would go about getting more information about applying for training at The Seeing Eye. I had wanted a guide dog for years, but somehow, something always seemed to be in the way.

I was a single mother, and when Polly, my daughter, was very young, my mother didn't think it was a great idea for me to be away from Polly for so long. Then when Polly got old enough that she could have been left, I was not in a place that would have been safe for me to work a dog. Nor did I go anyplace where I could work one, because I'd ended up where there was no public transportation.

Eventually, in 2005, I moved to a better location, to another apartment complex, where I lived until October of 2010. That was where I met Donnie, who was my neighbor. There, with his help, I rehabilitated myself a little. We dated the whole five years I lived there.

Rehabilitating myself meant that I needed to relearn some of what I'd forgotten when I had ended up in an apartment where I had no public transportation. I needed to relearn some cane skills. I had to learn how to navigate the bus system and basically get used to doing things I'd always done, but had forgotten over the years of living in an isolated location. It wasn't until then that I began to seriously consider getting a guide dog.

Suddenly, I knew I could wait no longer. I knew in my heart that definitely, without a doubt, it was time for me to take this step. I also knew without a doubt that The Seeing Eye was where I wanted to go to get my first guide dog. As I said, I'd had many different experiences with people and their guide dogs. I'd seen dogs and handlers from many different schools. But I knew in my heart of hearts, and also in my gut, that this was absolutely the right decision.

Part 1

How Campbell Retrieved My Life

Chapter 1

Preparing for The Seeing Eye

Once I realized that going to The Seeing Eye and getting a guide dog was what I truly wanted to do, there were a lot of things to do to make that happen. The first of those was applying for and getting accepted to the school. I contacted Phyllis and asked her what I needed to do to apply. She gave me their phone number and the name of the lady in charge of Graduate Services, and I began the task.

I contacted Pauline Alexander by email in late May of 2010, letting her know that I was interested in coming to the school and training to get a guide dog. She sent me an application to fill out; soon, I was on my way toward achieving my goal. After completing a lot of paperwork, I waited to hear from them. It seemed to take forever, but I know that in reality, it didn't take that long. I soon had an appointment set with one of their field reps. He was to come down and evaluate me to see if I qualified for training.

Finally that day arrived. When he came to my house, Emmy and Phyllis were with him. As she gave me a hug, Phyllis said, "Just here for support!" We talked for a while, and the rep asked me many questions. He asked me about my life, about things I normally did; I knew he was trying to get a better idea of what I did on a daily basis. That would help them to give me a dog that would be the best possible match.

Then we went outside, and he observed me cane traveling

to and from the bus stop down the street from my apartment. Then we did a Juno Walk. During a Juno Walk, an instructor has you take the harness handle, which they're holding, and walk with them to see how well you walk and how well you follow directions. This way, they can get an idea of your walking speed and how well you can sense direction.

Once that was done, there was nothing to do but wait until they called.

They contacted me near the end of 2010 to tell me they had a class date for me. They wanted me to come in January of 2011, but I had work obligations that I simply could not turn over to anyone else, so I was forced to turn them down. A couple of days later, they called back to say that they could have me come on April 2, and did I think that would work for me. I told them I would *make* it work.

As Ms. Alexander and I talked, I updated her concerning my living arrangements. I explained that Donnie (who was my fiancé at the time) and I had moved from the apartment complex where we'd been neighbors to a house where we were still neighbors, but sharing living expenses. I explained that we'd found a large, three-bedroom house with a second large, three-bedroom apartment up top, above the attached garage. I lived in the upper-level apartment, which included a raised deck.

I explained to her that my surroundings had also changed. This is more of a residential area, with houses, schools, churches, and even a neighborhood park. I told her there were multiple bus stops in the area for me to use, and I even told her about the little corner market that Donnie and I walked to sometimes.

It excited me to think what great and wondrous adventures awaited me, but to be honest, it also frightened me a bit. I had known that moving would change things for me, but I would learn that, in the end, it would indeed do huge things for my life.

I went to my supervisor, Lynn Sorrell, and spoke to him

about my needing a month off to go to Morristown, New Jersey to The Seeing Eye to get a guide dog. After much back and forth discussion between the two of us and a bit of strong encouragement from my coworker Dawn, we soon had an agreement in place. Donnie would take my place while I was gone. This would not only assure that the job would be done well in my absence, but it would also allow us to maintain the income we needed to continue to live in our home. Of course all this was a huge relief to me.

Then the real fun began. I had to have clothes, shoes, and even luggage so that I could make the trip properly. Donnie and I went clothes and shoe shopping, and my father took me to buy luggage. He wanted me to have a new set, so that traveling would be easier for me. At first, Dad was not very accepting of the idea of my going to get a guide dog. He had issues with my using a guide dog, because he just wasn't sure that it was as safe as everyone claimed. He'd seen up close how others worked a guide dog, but it had always been in a setting where there were plenty of other sighted people around. He had never really seen what a guide dog could do, so his fears were understandable. But he still made sure that I had all I needed to make my trip as successful as possible. That's how my dad has always done things, even when he hasn't always agreed with me. He has always made sure, whenever necessary and if at all possible, that I've had whatever I needed to be as successful as I could be. For that I will be forever grateful.

Once clothing, shoes, and luggage were secure, the next thing I needed to do was try to get in better physical shape. Since training was going to involve a lot of walking, I decided that walking each day would be a great way to begin. So walk I did. I had to start out slowly—or I should say, Donnie and I had to start out slowly. I couldn't walk anywhere much at all by myself with just my cane. Sure, I went places, but I went by myself only if those places were very close to the bus stop. So I needed Donnie to help with this portion of my pre-training.

Even though it seemed to me that Donnie and I walked a lot, it turned out that I still didn't have the stamina to walk long distances. I knew that training would involve quite a bit more walking, so I began to try to talk Donnie into increasing how much he and I walked. After a while, it began to get easier, and as time went along, I began to do better and better with how far I could walk.

But then we hit a real cold snap that lasted almost all through February and into the first part of March; this slowed us down quite a bit. I became slightly discouraged and didn't work as hard as I should have to continue what I had begun. Donnie didn't really push me very much, either. He didn't try to motivate me as much as he should have. Once I began training at the school, I would learn very quickly that this had been a mistake. It was not, however, one that I wouldn't be able to overcome.

Donnie and I had some personal issues. One of many was that he felt that I wouldn't need him anymore once I got home with my new guide dog. I was concerned about how he felt, but I couldn't really understand, so I called the school and spoke to someone in the training department about this. I learned that this was a common belief among blind people's partners, family members, and friends: those who had always had an active role in assisting their blind loved ones. I was encouraged to continue to assure Donnie that this would not be the case, but I was also encouraged to not let this cause me to change my mind.

In fact, on several occasions, I had almost done just that, but I finally realized that I absolutely had to go. I was tired of being a cane traveler, tired of always finding myself needing someone to help me get here or there, someplace that just wasn't cane accessible. I wanted the same independence that Phyllis had shown me while losing me in that mall. I was absolutely determined to make this happen—with or without Donnie's support.

Chapter 2

My Trip and Arrival

April 2, 2011 had finally arrived, and it was time to go. My dad was in the driveway, waiting for me. My luggage was loaded. I stood at the door with tears in my eyes, saying my goodbyes. On what should have been one of the most exciting days of my life, I was upset. It was because I'd asked Donnie to come with us to the airport, and he had refused. His excuse was that he had his son that weekend, and his son had a friend over. My dad had told us more than once that that would not be a problem; he'd even offered to take the boys and let them stand on the observation deck for a while after my plane left, so they could watch the planes take off and land. But Donnie still wouldn't go. I asked him why, but I never got what I considered a good answer.

There was nothing to do but go ahead and leave. So I wiped away my tears as best I could, said goodbye, and was on my way. I have to say that my dad was not really impressed with Donnie's lack of interest. Although he said nothing much about it, I knew my dad well enough to know that he didn't like it at all.

It would not be an easy trip. The first problem was that my flight from the Tri-Cities (Kingsport, Johnson City, and Bristol, Tennessee) to Charlotte, North Carolina was delayed, and my connecting flight had to be changed. When I arrived in Charlotte, I found that I'd missed my connecting flight and so was delayed again. For a while, due to all the confusion, even The Seeing Eye did not know exactly where I'd flown off to. I had forgotten to turn my cell phone back on while in the airport, so no one was able to reach me at all. At last I was in the air again and on the last leg of my journey to Newark, New Jersey.

When the plane landed, it was four hours past my originally scheduled arrival time, and I was exhausted and hungry. When the gate agent got me to the driver who was to take me to the school, I was immediately frustrated by the fact that she seemed to speak very little English. In addition, she seemed to remain on her cell phone almost the entire time we were together. I had very much wanted to stop for a bathroom break before leaving the airport, but I wasn't able to get her to understand that. I was never sure if it was because she didn't understand, or because she simply wasn't paying attention. But of course that immediately added to my stress.

Once at the school, the driver left me in the lobby and walked away. Soon the school nurse arrived and took me to my room. She set my luggage down, and before I could ask her where the bathroom was, she was gone, telling me as she left that my instructor was busy settling his other students upstairs, but that he would be with me shortly. This threw me a little, because I'd really expected to be met by my instructor when I got there. I felt that things were not as they should have been. Again, I felt frustrated. On top of that, I was beginning to feel that perhaps I'd made a mistake in coming at all. I was near tears and feeling very much out of my element.

Finally, out of pure desperation, I decided to get out my cane and explore the room, to see if I could locate the bathroom on my own. I found it at last, and had just come out when my instructor knocked on the door. He came in and introduced himself. He told me his name was Drew Gibbon and asked me if I was Patricia Fletcher. I told him I was and reached out to shake his hand.

As we shook hands, I staggered slightly as I stepped

forward. He reached out and steadied me and then gently sat me down in a chair, asking if I was all right. I told him I'd been gone from my house since 9:00 that morning, that I'd had nothing to eat all day except a can of Pringles and a beer on the plane, and that I was also in serious need of a smoke. He told me we were due in a meeting upstairs, but he promised food and coffee when we got there. I decided that was good enough for the moment. I stood up slowly, and taking his arm, I went willingly with him to the meeting.

Once upstairs, I was brought a very nice plate of supper and a big mug of good, hot, strong coffee. This did a lot to improve the way I felt. After the meeting was over, Drew took me back downstairs and explained that he needed to do another Juno Walk with me so he could get a better idea of me and how I walked—all before we began training the next day. He explained that even though I'd had a Juno Walk when I'd first been evaluated by the field rep, before I'd been accepted into training, he needed to walk with me himself. He wanted to evaluate me now that I'd been doing some walking and exercising. In turn, I explained to him that I had moved since the rep had been to see me. I told him about the nicer residential area I live in now, versus the apartment complex environment I'd been in when I'd been evaluated the first time.

Although I was really exhausted, I knew this had to be done. It wasn't Drew's fault that my fiancé was being an ass and had started me off upset, or that my plane had been late on both legs of my journey. Nor was it his fault that he hadn't been in the lobby when I had arrived. So I agreed with no argument.

We set out and soon discovered that I was having a problem with the difference between left and right. It seemed as though I had simply forgotten all I'd ever known about direction. As Drew took me through the building, teaching me the layout, he laughingly asked me if I'd forgotten to pack my sense of direction, and with a smile, he suggested I have someone get it to me via UPS. Even though he would tell me we were going to turn left and walk toward a specific place, when we repeated the exercise to see what happened when I directed him, as I would direct the dog, two out of three times, I would suggest right instead. We decided that it must be due to my being tired and stressed, and that we wouldn't worry about it too much that night.

However, even when we worked in town the next day, it was a problem. We learned later that this problem would never really go away. Drew tried several different things to try to help me with this issue, and although I found different coping skills during training, to this day, I have never found a way to completely eliminate the problem. No one ever spoke to me directly about this, in that no one voiced concerns that I might not be able to work a dog, but I am sure it was a worry to the training team during class.

After we'd completed the Juno Walk, Drew began to show me more about my room. He guided me around the room, describing everything in great detail. This did a lot to dispel my unease. As he explained to me what should be housed in various drawers and in the dresser, as well as on the top shelf of my closet, I began to plan out where I would keep things while I was there. This made me feel much more at home.

As I leaned over to see how the night stand was made, I nearly hit my head on the headboard of my bed. Drew quickly reached out and caught me. "Hey, lady!" he said. "Ya might want to watch that! You'll end up knocking yourself out cold, flat on the floor!" We laughed, and I asked him where I could go to smoke. He told me there was a smoking room upstairs and a patio downstairs, but that they were both located off the men's wing, and he wasn't sure if I could go there yet or not.

I folded my arms, turned to face him, stood as straight and tall as I could, and quickly and firmly informed him that should he decide there was nowhere for me to smoke, he would very quickly learn that he would not enjoy having me as a student. I had the feeling he was messing with me, but I was starting to feel a bit frazzled and wasn't having it. Amazingly enough, he did find a place for me to smoke, but it wasn't in either of the designated areas. After finally having a smoke, and then going to the lounge on my floor to get a drink, I decided I'd simply had enough for one day and went to get ready for bed. I knew the next day would be very busy, so I decided that sleep was my best option.

As I was getting things unpacked and getting ready for bed, Drew knocked on my door and asked if I was settling in all right. I told him I was feeling a bit anxious and overwhelmed. He stood and talked with me for a bit while I finished settling things in my room, and his gentle manner began to put me even more at ease. I found him to be very patient, kind, and understanding. As I unpacked my medications, he asked a few questions, which I happily answered. When I had filled out my application, I'd also let them know about my bipolar disorder and fibromyalgia. I felt that it was important for them to know all they could about me. This was so they could make the best match possible for me where a dog was concerned; also, my instructor would know all he or she would need to know in order to make my training go as smoothly as possible.

I explained to him about my bipolar disorder and what that entailed. I didn't go into great detail, but I did explain about mood swings and what things would trigger them. I also explained about the pain my fibromyalgia caused me. As it turned out, we would have another, more involved discussion about all these things later; but my fear that he would not understand was quickly dissipated by the way he handled the information I gave him. He did not seem to be at all put off by anything I told him, and it seemed that in fact he understood pretty well what I was saying.

All this was a huge relief to me, and I found that being able to chat with him a bit went a long way toward helping me through that first night. Not only did having him know these things about me make me feel better, but it helped me to trust him and feel safe with him, and those two things were very important for me. Over the years, I have sometimes had bad experiences in blind institution settings. Drew would not only be in charge of my training; in many ways, he would also be in charge of my care. Thus it was very comforting to me to have him understand and make me feel safe and secure, and that did indeed help throughout my training.

Chapter 3

April 4, 2011

Dog Day: The Most Wonderful Day Ever

The next day, I would meet my guide dog. As the evening before Dog Day wound down, I was more wired than ever and sat outside until the security guard came to lock the patio door. While I was pacing the halls later, Drew popped out of his room and asked me what was bothering me. I told him I couldn't settle down, because I kept thinking about all the things I needed to know for the point at which he would put a leash in my hand with a guide dog attached to the other end. He walked me back to my room, saying, "You know all you need to know for now, for when I first give you your dog."

"But there are so many things to remember! What if…?"

He gently interrupted me. "Honey, listen. At first, the most important things you're going to need to know are right here in your heart." He spoke reassuringly to me as we stopped in front of my room. "You have the ability to love, and in the beginning, that will be enough. And as you begin to learn what to do to work with your dog, it will still be one of the most important things you will ever need to know. Now try to get yourself to bed and get some sleep."

He wished me a good night and went whistling down the hall. Over the next month, I would come to be very annoyed by that whistle on many occasions.

***

Finally Dog Day arrived. I had been asked to wait in my room, but I felt so nervous that I ignored Drew's request altogether and went to a friend's door. We eased our stress by talking about what breed of dog we might get and how we liked interesting names. We both loved dogs and wanted to give them the love that would encourage them to love us back. Suddenly I realized I'd been gone a little longer than I'd meant to, so I went back to my room with my mind spinning with excitement and fear.

To calm myself, I reminisced about other dogs in my life. Rowdy was a rescue dog that had been with me for 14 years before I lost my sight. He was a black-and-white Beagle mix and only eight months old when he was found in a January snowstorm along the side of the Interstate. Someone had lost him, I was pretty sure, because he had a Santa collar on. So I took him home. He was as sweet as the day was long but had a lot of energy, thus the name Rowdy. He grabbed my heart, and I still miss him. I wondered if I could love this guide dog as much as I had loved Rowdy, and for just a moment or so, I felt guilty for even trying.

Donnie, my fiancé, had Cassie, an elderly miniature poodle, and we had rescued a dog named Rocky in February of 2011. But I hadn't had a dog of my very own to love and care for since Rowdy had crossed the Rainbow Bridge and had gone over to the other side, where all is peace and love. My guess is that Rowdy still tosses in a few antics just for fun.

Wrapped up in my thoughts of Rowdy, Cassie, Rocky, and how I might react to a guide dog, I forgot where I was for a moment. I know that sounds crazy, but to this day, I really don't have the right words to describe what I was feeling. I felt happy, excited, honored, and terrified all at the same time.

There was a knock at my door. I said "Come in!" more

loudly than I had meant to, but Drew came in quietly with a dog walking beside him. My excitement didn't seem to faze Drew at all. I suppose he sees a lot of that, and he probably thought nothing of it. However, I was noticing everything.

Drew placed the leash in my hand and said, "Patty, this is Campbell, C a m p b e l l." His spelling the name was helpful to me, because I don't spell all that well, due to my always reading audio books.

I knelt down on the floor next to the finest big dog I'd ever had my hands on. As soon as Drew gave me the leash, I began to pet Campbell and had a strong desire to know all there was to know about him. I hadn't realized just how much I had missed having a dog of my own.

As I felt this big dog all over, Drew described him as a 67-pound black Labrador Retriever. Campbell licked my face and then put his big mouth around my arm and chewed gently on it. It was both wonderful and frightening all at the same time.

As he headed toward the door, Drew said, "I'm going to give you two some time to get to know one another."

I turned to him and asked a bit nervously, "You're leaving me alone with him already? What if he gets really upset or something?" As I spoke, Campbell began to mouth me in earnest, and slobber began to drip down my arm. "W...W...What do I do with *this*...?"

Drew chuckled to himself as he opened the door and stepped out.

"You'll figure it out," he said, "and I'll be back later to check on you. Enjoy!" With that, he walked out the door, whistling yet again. At that moment, I wasn't annoyed; I couldn't have cared less about Drew Gibbon or anyone else in the world. My hands and being were all about Campbell.

Once I determined that this big dog wasn't going to eat me, Campbell sat quietly and let me explore his body. I felt his muscles and his head, looked inside his mouth, and smelled his ears. Yes, I smelled his ears! People kidded me for doing that, since he'd just come from the groomer, but it turned out that that was a good thing. When I went to a lecture later on during training, one on teeth and ear cleaning, they told us that we had to get to know how our dogs' ears smelled, what their teeth felt like, and all sorts of other things I needed to know.

Time wasn't moving for me as I sat on the floor, petting and talking to Campbell. Even as trained as he was, he was trying to accept a new person into his life. If he heard a noise in the hall, he would get distracted and whine, probably for Drew. I snuggled him close to me, telling him in a soothing voice that he was safe in my loving hands. As the afternoon went on, he began to trust me. We both had a lot of love and faithfulness to give. My heart opened to him and his to me. Then and still today, I knew and know that a dog, either guide or pet, requires love and reassurance just as any other living being does.

Chapter 4

The Connection and That First Walk

I'm not sure how much time passed while Campbell and I sat in each other's arms, getting to know one another. I couldn't tell you when Drew knocked on my door and came back into my room. It seemed to me that Campbell and I had escaped into our own private world, and that for us, no other people or animals existed.

After some time, I began to come back to myself and my surroundings. I realized that Drew was there and raised my head, then turned to him as if returning from a long distance. With tears in my eyes, I said, "It's as if I've loved him forever." I still had one arm wrapped snugly around Campbell; it was as if I were afraid that if I let go, he'd disappear.

I could hear the emotion in Drew's voice when he said, "I'm pretty sure it's the same for him."

We stayed like that for a moment. I was on the floor, one arm wrapped around Campbell, and Drew was standing a few feet away, watching us. It was simply a moment I wasn't quite ready to let go of. As I held Campbell in the crook of my arm, the energy I felt from him was unlike anything I'd ever felt before. I could feel his longing for Drew. I could also feel his wanting to love me, but being frightened to do so.

I could also feel Drew's energy. It, too, was rather scattered. I could feel his love for Campbell, but I could also feel his hope that this match would work. Friends and neighbors, I simply can't describe that moment any other way than to say that for a moment, brief though it was, there was a triangle of connection, linking Campbell, Drew, and me.

Drew shattered the spell. "What do you know about harnessing the dog?" he asked.

I stood and took the harness from him. In fact, I did know something about this. Phyllis had made sure to teach me how to put the harness on and take it off. She had said that she didn't want me to go to class not knowing anything at all. I remember that it felt good to know *something* in this new world, where it was becoming increasingly obvious that I really knew next to nothing.

Drew went over all the parts of the harness with me and made sure I understood their functions. Then, once I had put my handsome boy in his harness correctly, we were ready to begin.

As we started out the door, Drew suggested that I simply heel Campbell through the doorway, so as not to set him up to fail right away with me. He explained that if Campbell should accidentally run me into the door frame while going through the door, he would need to be corrected, and he didn't want that to be the case with us this soon. I agreed and did as he suggested; I heeled Campbell through the doorway. But to Campbell, it was business all the way. He did such a good job bringing me through that doorway that he might as well have been working. I fairly cheered going into the hall, saying, "Yay, Campbell! Good boy!" Drew walked behind me; he seemed to be amused by my happiness regarding how we had gone through that doorway.

As we started down the hallway, he instructed me to pick up the harness handle. As I did so, I instinctively reached out with my right hand and touched the wall, then began to trail it, as I'd always done. Drew immediately removed my hand from the wall. Putting it firmly back at my side, he said sternly, "No! Don't do that! You'll encourage him to run you into things if you do!"

This stopped me in my tracks. I turned and looked up at him. With my eyes starting to fill with tears and my lip trembling, I said, "But Mr. Gibbon, if I don't touch the wall, I can't see where I'm going!"

He took what I'm sure was a steadying breath to keep from laughing, and then said more gently, "Honey, that's what the dog is for."

I can still almost swear that I heard a door close softly somewhere down the main hall, and that laughter ensued shortly thereafter. I guess now that I look back on it, it was kind of funny, but at the time, I didn't find it funny at all.

***

By the time we had made our way out onto the Leisure Path, I had begun to feel a bit out of sorts. I was not at all sure that I knew what I was doing. Nothing felt in place for me. I didn't feel as if my feet were working right, and soon I simply felt completely lost and a bit off balance. Drew had been walking slightly ahead of me so he could keep an eye on his other three students, as well as me, but suddenly he dropped back beside me.

"What's wrong?" he asked. At some point, he must have seen the confusion on my face.

I stood there a moment, trying to gather my thoughts.

"Well, things feel a bit off balance to me. I know this shouldn't be any different than walking sighted guide with someone. Or should it?" I sighed and dropped my hands to my sides. I didn't understand at all what I was feeling.

Drew, however, did not seem one bit upset about this. I suppose he hears stuff like this all the time.

"Just pay attention to how Campbell's gait feels beside you. Think about getting yourself into rhythm with him, just as you would fall in step when taking someone's arm to walk."

I thought about that for a minute, then started Campbell and myself going again. After a bit, things began to feel a little better.

"Better?" Drew asked.

"Yes!" I answered excitedly. I felt lots better. After walking a bit more, I was just about to say, "Look, Mom! No elbow!" when I lost my footing and tripped.

Drew came back to me. After making sure I was okay, while helping me to my feet, he said, "Okay, lady, shake it off! That's fall one of one thousand." Then he handed me a tissue and simply walked away.

Finally, Campbell and I had made it all the way around the Leisure Path. I'm not sure how long that path actually is, but to me, it seemed to go on for miles. I had a lot of different feelings during that first walk, but I have yet to find the words to adequately describe the feeling of freedom I got when I walked around that path with no one guiding me, just me and my dog. There has never been another feeling quite like that one. It was, and I believe still is, the closest I'll get to sight in this lifetime.

Chapter 5

Hell Week

As the first few days of training went along, I found out that there were lots of things I didn't know anymore, things that I had thought I knew. The first thing that really floored me was how walking in traffic had changed since I'd been doing a whole lot of it years before. I didn't understand all I thought I did about traffic flow and surge. I didn't know about turning lanes the way others did. I just felt very much out of my comfort zone. As time went along, though, I began to pick up more and more.

Drew Gibbon, I have to say, turned out to be the most patient man I've ever worked with in my life. He never made me feel stupid or belittled me when I didn't understand something. If I showed any sign of feeling unsure, he encouraged me, saying, "You're not expected to know everything all at once. If that were so, we wouldn't need four weeks to train you." He would also say to me in a deep Yankee accent, "Don't worry about it, lady." That used to always make me laugh.

The end of the first week finally arrived, and we did our first solo trip. Drew had partnered me with a lady in our group who had had guide dogs before; she was there getting a successor. I was to follow her but make decisions on my own about things. However, I felt really afraid. So, as much as I could, I followed her. This caused me a problem at one point, and I ended up in a flower bed. Drew came along and spoke to me, but at first, I wasn't sure who he was. There I was, in this ridiculous flower bed, not exactly sure where I was, and he walked up; in this deep Brooklyn accent, he said, "Lady, what ya doing in that nice lady's flowers?"

At first I didn't recognize him and wished the ground would swallow me up. Then I grinned and said, "Just following my dog, sir." He laughed and explained that my partner's dog had cut the corner too short, but that they had corrected and gone on. Campbell, however, followed my body language, and so we ended up in the flowers instead of turning the corner and continuing. As he helped me out of the flower bed, Drew gently but firmly said, "Don't rely so much on others. Trust yourself and your dog."

I finished the rest of the trip with no problem, but I was down on myself for not getting that one part right. When we got back to the school, Jeff, our class supervisor, met us in the lobby.

"How was your solo?" he asked me.

I frowned. "Horrible."

Drew quickly spoke up and said, "It wasn't nearly as bad as she imagines." He turned to me and said, "Go get cleaned up for lunch and stop worrying so much. Hell, if you already knew everything you needed to know, I wouldn't have to be here."

I heard Jeff and Drew talking together as I walked away, but they had turned away from me, so I couldn't hear that much of what they were saying. I did hear Drew say one thing that made me start thinking a bit differently. That was, "I really wish she believed in herself a little more." It made me feel good that someone thought I was worth believing in.

That afternoon, I passed Jeff again in the hall as Campbell and I were going toward the stairs. He asked me how I was doing. I told him I felt as though I finally had the hang of it. He laughed and said, "That won't last long. Next week's Hell Week."

I turned to him and said, "Nah, I think I really am getting the hang of it."

"Talk to me again about Wednesday," he said.

I didn't understand then what he meant, but I soon would. Sunday was uneventful, but Monday was hard, and the whole week ended up being that way.

First off, the weather was horrible. It rained every day and never seemed to let up. Even if the rain wasn't so terribly heavy, there always seemed to be a mist, and the wind was always blowing. By the end of that week I was sore all over, had blisters on my feet, and was sick to death of rain. Training was sometimes just short of brutal. We were up and moving by 5:30 in the morning most days, and some days, we didn't get done until almost 9:00 p.m. It was physically and emotionally exhausting, and there were times when I simply didn't think I would be able to go one step further.

At times, Drew could be as bad as a drill sergeant trying to get green Army boys ready for war. I certainly don't mean to say that he was ever mean, but he was hardnosed at times about training. When you were out there on the streets, learning some of the most important things you would ever learn in your entire life, he didn't play. He tried whenever possible to make things as fun and enjoyable as possible, but there were many times when he simply meant business, and there was no room for much more.

***

One afternoon during a training trip, I tripped for the third time over this huge crack in the sidewalk. I landed in a puddle, of all things, and somehow, that was the last straw for me. I'd been kind of whiny all day; I hadn't felt like much of anything, either emotionally or physically. So that particular fall hit me harder than the rest.

I sat for a minute. The fall had made my teeth click together, and I'd bitten my tongue. I was near tears. Drew gently reached for my hand.

"Come on, honey," he said. "Let's go back to the school and get cleaned up before supper."

I cut him off and pushed his hand away. "I can't do this anymore!" I yelled. "I'm tired, cold, and wet, and I just don't..." I faded off before finishing my sentence, then sat with my face in my hands, crying.

Drew stepped back and took a long look at me. He took a deep breath and said in a deep, firm voice that I had never heard him use before, "Okay, young lady! Let's get you back to the school, and I'll make arrangements to send you home."

I realized that he meant it, and that I wouldn't be able to take Campbell with me. I wasn't far enough along in the training. I suddenly felt so very guilty, angry, and upset. All those feelings were running around in my head at once, along with the echo of his voice.

I wiped my tears angrily from my face. I stood up slowly and got hold of Campbell's harness. I looked at Drew and said, "To heck with that shit, Yankee!" Then I turned Campbell and myself around and started to the training lounge. I beat Drew by a couple of minutes, and thanks to someone letting me in, I was inside getting something warm to drink by the time he came in. No doubt he was actually right behind me all the time, but he had let me beat him to help increase my confidence.

I ran over to him and threw my arms around him, saying, "What took ya so long, slowpoke Yankee?" He laughed and held me back away from him so he could look at me. As he wiped a smudge of dirt from my face, he said, "You're doing a great job! Keep it up."

We went back to school, then had supper and a short lecture. For once, I took Drew's advice and didn't argue when he told me to get to bed early and get some rest. I took a hot bath, then got into bed with a book.

About an hour and a half later, Drew knocked on my door, then looked in on me and Campbell. Campbell was snoozing in his crate, and I was curled up with my book.

"Don't read too late," Drew said. "Busy, busy day tomorrow."

I yawned and said, "This ain't Guide Dog School; this is boot camp for blind people."

He laughed. "Get some sleep! I don't wanna have to come and drag you out tomorrow, but I will if you're not out before first light."

I fell asleep that night feeling that I just might make it through. Having Mr. Drew Gibbon as an instructor simply didn't leave room for much else. He was determined to make a guide dog handler out of me. He knew exactly when to really get on my ass, when to be easy on me, and how to make me laugh. So I was just about ready to believe he might pull it off.

I know without a doubt that Drew more than earned his pay with that class. I was not at all an easy student. I could be very emotional: happy one minute, then crying the next, and when I wasn't in one of those two states, he was pulling me back from someone or something that had angered me in some way. He would take those moments, no matter how difficult they must have been for him, too, and turn them into teachable moments.

He talked to me about how my emotions would travel down the leash to Campbell. He explained further that when he and others said things about watching my emotions while handling Campbell, they weren't just trying to sound superior. He gave me examples, and he pointed out different things to me regarding Campbell's reactions.

He had his work cut out for him, for sure, but he didn't seem to be about to give up on me. So I decided that if he believed I could do it, I would try. Suddenly, I very much wanted to be successful, and I very much wanted to make Drew proud of me, as well.

Chapter 6

Learning the Hard Way

On Friday of that horrible week, we all got together upstairs in the common lounge after lecture. There was one student playing the guitar and another playing the piano, and some of us were singing. I had bought a six-pack of beer, and another student had brought some wine from home. It was homemade wine, and so even though I'd already had two beers, I decided I'd try the wine. I felt okay, not even the least bit tipsy. I had gotten up to get both beers, so I felt okay to drink some wine.

Well, when we went to pour it, we realized that we had only tumbler-sized plastic glasses, the kind that soda would go in at a picnic. But that didn't stop us; no way! We were celebrating getting through one of the hardest weeks we would face, and we were all hyper and happy. I, for one, was not thinking about later on, about what consequences there might be as a result of my decision to drink wine out of a glass meant for soda, one that probably held something like 12 or 16 ounces.

Well, the wine was so very good that I decided that if one glass was good, another had to be better. Drew and other instructors had been coming and going, in and out of the lounge all evening. Eventually, Drew stopped by my table.

"I believe you've had about enough, young lady."

I looked up at him and laughed. "Aw, come on! I'm okay to operate my canine!"

He stood quietly for a minute, and then said, "Okay, let's see you walk."

I laughed again. "I don't know who ya think you're talkin' to, Yankee. I can drink with the best of 'em." I was, however, starting to feel a little lightheaded and just a little too warm. I stood up and leaned over to reach for Campbell's harness. As I did, I just kept going. I went right on over, ass over tea kettle.

Drew laughed; I'm sure he couldn't help it. He reached down to help me up. "So, you can drink with the best of them, huh? Looks like you can fall with the best of them, too."

I sat there for a minute. Then, very determinedly, I said, "Well, wait a minute. Let me get my balance. I can do this." I tried to get my feet under me, but the shoes I had on were the kind that you were supposed to exercise in; they had rocker bottoms on them. Drew had helped me pick them out a couple of days before. Buying those shoes had been one of the worst mistakes of my life, but I had refused to admit it, because I was embarrassed. I still denied it even when Sue, another instructor, teased me about them, saying, "So when I see you lying on your bed with your feet propped on the headboard, it's not because those shoes are killing you?"

In the meantime, I couldn't manage to get and stay on my feet. Drew laughed so hard he sounded as though he might cry.

"Come on, redneck, time for you to get to bed."

He helped me up and led me down the hall, telling me to heel my dog. He was still laughing when we got to the elevator. He had decided there was no way he was taking me down two flights of stairs. At that time, the elevator was one that looked as though it been around since World War Two. It was pretty small, and it had one of those metal gates that close in front of you, so Drew, Campbell, and I couldn't all fit in there.

Drew put Campbell and me inside and closed us up. He told me he'd meet me downstairs. He started the elevator and sent us on our way, then ran down the stairs to meet us. On his way down, though, he ran into someone and started talking to them.

Campbell's Rambles

In the meantime, the elevator had come to the first floor and stopped, but I had no idea how to get out. I was starting to not feel so hot, and I could hear Drew and the person he'd run into out there talking.

I knocked on the wall beside me. "Hello? I want out!"

Drew called to me. "Hmm? I have you right where I want you now, ha, ha!" He laughed an evil-sounding laugh.

I knocked again. I was starting to really feel the effects of the alcohol, and I wanted to go to my room. "Please? Let me *out*!" I was sweating and starting to feel more than a little upset.

Drew came quickly and opened the door. "It's okay," he said gently. "I'm just messin' with you. Here, take my arm."

He continued to keep his voice low and calm and gently placed my right hand in the crook of his elbow. He led me and Campbell out of the elevator and down to our room. We passed his room and went on down the hall to mine. At the door, he asked me if I was okay.

Feeling a bit out of sorts, I said, "I think so...."

He opened the door, and Campbell and I stepped through.

"Goodnight," I said, turning away from him. I was crying, and I didn't know why. I felt emotionally disoriented.

He laid a gentle hand on my arm. "Get some sleep. Early day tomorrow, and you, young lady, have had just a little too much to drink."

I smiled a bit and wiped my eyes. Turning toward him, I said, "What was your first clue?" He gave me a gentle push on into the room.

"Goodnight. See you in the morning. Don't make me come get you," he teased, shutting the door as he walked away.

***

When I woke, I had one of the most horrible hangovers I've ever had. Between the beer and wine, plus my nighttime

45

medication and the pizza I'd eaten, I could barely stand the smell of Campbell's food when I gave him his breakfast.

The next problem was getting him out to park time and then getting myself able to go to breakfast. I could not imagine eating; that just seemed like a very bad idea, and as I thought about it, I suddenly felt very sick. Campbell was eating, and I stepped into the bathroom to see if I could just wash my face a little and catch my breath.

I finally got myself together, and then I heard them paging me. I was late getting Campbell outside, and I knew I'd better step it up if I didn't want to be in trouble. I made my way down to the park area.

As I stepped outside, Drew called to me. "Hey, how ya doing this morning?"

I put my hand up and said, "Shhh! Not so loud, please!"

He laughed, and so did the rest of the instructors standing beside him. One of the others called to me. "Rough night?"

I just smiled and said, "Don't wanna talk about it."

Everyone around me laughed, and I simply went on with what I was doing, hoping I could get done and back to my room without passing out or throwing up right there in the middle of all those dogs doing their business. At last Campbell was done, and I realized I was going to have to pick up after him. Now, I pride myself on the fact that nothing much at all bothers my stomach. But that's under normal circumstances, and there was not one thing normal about how I was feeling on this morning of hangover horrors.

I held my breath, put the bag on my hand, and leaned over to pick up Campbell's leavings. To this day, I do not know how on earth I managed to keep from being sick. Before that day, I had never had anything bother me as much as picking up after Campbell did. I held my breath as I picked it up, thanking all the gods and goddesses in the universe and beyond for plastic baggies. Somehow I managed to get it picked up and bagged and in the trash—or the "honey pot," as we lovingly called it—and then got back inside and up to my room.

Drew found me there, lying in bed, hidden under the covers. He knocked on the door, and I softly said, "Come in."

He opened the door just a little and asked me if I was okay. I peeked my head out from under the covers and told him I thought I'd have to rest and get better before I could die.

He laughed. "Twenty minutes till breakfast!"

I sat up, "Breakfast? Sir, you don't really think I'm going to eat, do you?"

He was not laughing when he said, "You'd best try, young lady! You're scheduled to go out on First Trip this morning."

Now I was horrified. "First Trip?" I sat there curled up in the middle of my bed, holding onto my covers. "First Trip?" I repeated.

"Yes, young lady, First Trip, and don't be late!"

"Sir...?" I called after him, but he shut the door and walked away, once again whistling that annoying little whistle. I don't think he even knows he does that, but I cannot be the only one who notices or hates it.

As the sound of his whistling went away down the hall, I leaned over the side of the bed, picked up one of my shoes, and threw it at the door after him. "Damn stupid Yankee! Breakfast and First Trip? Seriously?"

I lay back down and pulled the covers back over my head, trying to will myself well. I have to laugh now when I think back to that morning. I really did feel awful, but I did end up getting up and going to breakfast, and I did end up going out on First Trip. I never have been sure how I got through that morning, but I can sure tell you how glad I was to know that my normally kind and caring instructor, who had suddenly turned into a mean, unfeeling, horrible monster, would be getting off duty at 12:00 and going away.

He cut me no slack that entire morning, and the one and

only time I complained about it, all he had to say was, "You will either learn to be more careful about when and how much you drink, or you'll pay the consequences for your irresponsibility. Now back to it, young lady." And that was that. That's just how he did things. You could play and kid around with him, but training was training, and you either had your shit together or you didn't make it in his world.

Part 2

The Home Stretch

Chapter 7

Halfway

As the next few days passed, we all began to really buckle down. There was a lot to learn, and time was growing short. It seemed as though we never slowed down. Yeah, I got a break here and there, but even if I wasn't out on a trip, it seemed to me that everything that happened all day long every day, even when I was on my own, was training. It was fantastic and horrible all at the same time. One minute I felt absolutely on top of the world, as though I could handle anything that Drew and the rest of the team could toss my way. The next, I felt as though I'd had the wind knocked out of me, and was once again almost ready to call it quits.

I cannot tell you exactly what those next few days were like for me. Due to the stress of it, as well as the fact that I wasn't sleeping well, due to the lack of certain medications that I could not use during training, along with the severe morning side effects, such as nausea and fatigue, I began to rapid cycle. Rapid cycling is when someone with bipolar disorder begins to experience extremely rapid mood swings. Sometimes they can be so severe that a person's moods can change several times during one day. At times, I was experiencing that. I tried very hard to keep it to myself. I'd been rejected from other training programs because of mental illness, and I was frightened of having the same issue here.

It was very difficult, since pretty much everything I was

doing was not only physical, but highly emotional, as well. Drew and the other staff were extremely helpful during those times when I simply could not hide things. Although I never actually sat down with Drew or others and explained about rapid cycling, how it worked and what caused it, for fear of being sent home, I did at times share with Drew how I was feeling—that is, whether I was anxious, excited, or happy. I never really went into detail, though, about what made me appear to always be on an emotional roller coaster.

When I did share something with him, he always listened and tried to understand, and he always encouraged me. Never at any time did he make me feel that I was doing something wrong. Never before, in any institutional setting, had I had anyone be as kind, caring, and patient a teacher as he was. How he kept from losing his temper with me, when I always had some smart-assed remark to make, I'll never know. Oh, don't get me wrong. He made it very clear from the beginning what he would and wouldn't tolerate, but he wasn't abusive about it, and that was new to me in many ways.

I remember learning the lesson of what he would and would not tolerate literally on the first trip out after getting Campbell. I remember making some offhanded, loudmouthed remark to a driver as he cut across in front of us. Not knowing all I thought I knew, of course I had something loud and rude to say.

Drew didn't say anything to me until we reached the opposite side of the street. Once we were on the sidewalk again, he called me to the side of the group and said, "You're too much of a nice and respectable young lady to act that way, and I think you can do better. Let's give that a try, okay?" He explained what the driver had done and why, then sent me back to the group with a final warning to watch that behavior.

I didn't make the same mistake twice. Not because he frightened me, not because he made me feel bad, and not because he belittled me, but because he expected better of me. He made me feel as though I could behave like somebody. He let me know that that was what he expected and that he wouldn't have it any other way.

It was something I'd never gotten before from anyone who was in authority in a training setting, so it was a really positive experience. Having someone like him, someone with 30 years of experience with this type of work, think I was worth something—well, it went a long way toward making me feel worthwhile, and as though I might really be successful with this.

I never knew whether he truly understood what an impact his work with me had on my entire life thereafter. We never got a chance to talk about it. My hope is that the things written in this book will help him realize that.

***

While going through training, I had many different experiences. Most of them were wonderful, and they're things I will never forget.

One of the things I'll never forget—or rather, one of the people—was Devin. He was one of my classmates, and he would turn out to be one of my very favorites. He was much younger than I was, in college, and doing a lot of things I'd always dreamed of doing. He too was a first-time guide dog handler, and it was wonderful to have someone along for the ride who understood some of what I was dealing with. Oh, sure, the retrains also knew what it was like to be new and green and not know a damned thing, but they had their own set of problems going on at the moment, and there were times when having a new handler around had to be really stressful for them.

Having Devin to talk to from time to time was very helpful. We would sometimes end up out on the smoking patio together. Devin didn't smoke. Well, that is to say, he didn't keep cigarettes, but if he took a notion, he would smoke one occasionally, so there were times when he'd come out and we would smoke and talk together. Devin had plans to study psychology, and I could see why. He had a lot of patience with people, was a good listener, and seemed to understand a wide range of things, even though he was quite young. I was impressed with the mixture in his personality of maturity and the ability to kick back and have some fun. I remember very well how he used to encourage me to just relax and enjoy what was happening to me. A lot of the time, what he told me worked and worked well.

It was nice having the older students around, too. Sometimes I would ask one or the other of them what they thought about something, or maybe I'd get an idea from them of how to do something. It seemed that everyone you ran into—staff, student, retired instructor, or volunteer—had something they could pass along to you that would help toward your being a success at the end of class. The whole time I was there, I never ceased being amazed by all the things I was learning, as well as by the speed at which I was beginning to adapt to the switch from being a long-time cane user to being a guide dog handler.

***

One quiet Sunday morning, I went into the women's lounge on my floor to get a cup of coffee. The weather had turned cold, with strong winds. I'd been out on the smoking patio having a cigarette and wanted to warm up. Sue and one of her students were sitting at the table talking, and I stopped to say hi. I'd met Sue the day after arriving, quite by accident. I had been coming up from the park area after having a cigarette, and she had stopped me in the hallway to ask why I'd been down there. We didn't have dogs, yet, so I guess she saw no reason for it.

I told her that Drew had sent me there to smoke. She asked

why, and I explained that he'd told me the night before that there were smoking areas, but that they were on the men's wing, and he hadn't yet found out if I could go down there. She made a noise of disgust and said, "Oh, Drew just doesn't want you to smoke. Come with me. I'll show you where to go." And that's what she did.

Now I stopped a few feet away from the table and said hi. Sue turned from talking with her student and invited me to join them. I told her I hadn't meant to interrupt, but that I guessed I could hang out for a minute. I tended to spend a lot of my free time in my room. I had several fears that made it difficult for me to be out and about with other students and in the common areas, so I just stuck to the first floor whenever I could.

As I settled Campbell under the table, Sue asked me if he was really my first guide dog. I laughed and told her that yes, Campbell was my very first ever guide.

"I would never have believed it if you hadn't told me," she said. "Drew told me that he was your first, but you seem to have it pretty together and have a really good idea of what you're doing."

I sat for a minute, not sure of how to respond. The student Sue had been talking to was new, and she didn't appear to be as adjusted to dog handling yet as I was, so I didn't want to offend her in any way.

"Well," I said, "I've owned and handled dogs since I was in my teens."

The girl sitting at the table with us asked, "If this is your first guide, how could you have handled dogs since your teens?"

I simply explained that I had owned dogs since my teen years, and that I'd been the one who was mostly responsible for their care. I went on to explain that even though guide dogs required a different type of handling, for the most part, the basics for all dogs were the same. I went on to say that I was hoping to use the things I was learning in training with our other pet dogs when I returned home.

Sue asked me some other questions about my experiences with dogs. She also asked a couple of questions about the dogs I had at home. This made me a little uncomfortable for two reasons. First of all, Rocky was a bit out of control where some aspects of his behavior were concerned, and it worried me that if they knew about this, they might be afraid that Campbell would key into them and that it could compromise his training. Then there was Cassie. She really needed to be put to sleep, but Donnie wouldn't hear of that. I was very worried that somehow they would learn of this and think that if I allowed her to live that way, I might also allow Campbell to live that way.

But I answered Sue's questions. In turn, I asked her a few about guide dog work. Before the lunch announcement, I had made another instructor friend and had found another place to get information.

***

I want to stop here and take a moment to clarify what I mean by instructor friend. Over the last two and a half years that I've been home with Campbell, I've learned that there are very good reasons for not becoming too involved with Seeing Eye staff after coming home. So what I mean by instructor friend is this. You can, at times, be a distant friend; maybe you can friend your instructor on Facebook. Obviously, if they're on Facebook, they're public and don't mind being contacted. But it isn't really advised to write them or call them at the school unless it concerns something extremely important regarding the wellbeing of the guide dog team. There are good reasons for this.

The best advice I can give you, whether you're a first-time student or a long-time grad going into class as a retrain, is to remember that first and foremost, you're there to receive training and instruction. Along with your dog, before you leave the school, you are there to learn to the best of your ability how to handle your dog and work it. Once you go home, your goal then becomes learning to handle and work that dog as independently as possible.

In short: Don't ever mix up friendship with a staff member's job.

I'm not saying that these people don't care for us; they obviously do, or they wouldn't be doing that type of work. But they're not our best friends. They're our trainers, our advisers, our go-to people when we find ourselves having dog-related issues. But to repeat: They are not our best friends, and they should never be put in the position of feeling that the students expect them to be that.

If you are fortunate enough to become friends on any level with any staff member, then you and that staff member should have a discussion about what is and is not appropriate for the two of you. You, as the student, should always remember what I previously stated: First and foremost, these people's job is to train us to handle our dogs to the very best of our ability.

From all the places I have ever received services, I have never received such great after-care as I have from The Seeing Eye. But there was a time when I took advantage of that. As you continue to read this book and the one that will follow it, *The Raw Truth*, you'll learn that I allowed things that were happening in my personal life to cloud my judgment. I didn't communicate well what I thought or felt, and in the end, I caused myself and others some problems.

It was a mistake that will most likely never be made right. The guilt from having made that mistake will haunt me for the rest of my life. There's no way to get closure, no way to apologize. So please understand the reasons for my writing this book.

Of course I've written the book to show how wonderfully

having a guide dog has changed my life, to show the absolute wonderment of the freedom I felt when taking that first walk, a freedom I still feel today. However, I also want to show how easy it is to get mixed up regarding how you feel about your connection with staff, to show what a bad idea this can be.

Last but not least, I want to show that I've learned a painful lesson in the process, that I've learned some important things about myself and those around me. I hope that students and staff alike will take this to heart, that they will help me to help others to never experience anything but the pure joy of what they come to The Seeing Eye to learn. That unique combination of training, learning, and first bonding with Campbell was and is the best thing to ever happen to me.

If I could say one thing to Drew and the rest of my team, other than thanks for an absolutely wonderful period of learning and personal growth, it would be, "Please forgive my shortcomings. Try to remember the happiness I used to help to spread, and the funny things I used to say. Please remember that joy you witnessed when you saw me and Campbell together."

At times, the things I write from here on out will be difficult for me, but I hope to share both the joy and sorrow that the last two and a half years have brought to me. I hope to let you know that no matter your circumstances, you can rise above them and move forward with your life. Don't allow anyone to be in control of you, and don't be afraid to speak up when you need help or if you're unsure of what someone else thinks or feels about you.

Chapter 8

The Mall

As we started down the home stretch toward the end of class, we began to take what are called Freelance Trips. For these trips, the instructor takes the student out and works on areas that the student has expressed a particular interest in, or perhaps it's something the student feels might present a particular problem when he or she returns home. So the student and instructor spend time working on these issues.

One thing I had expressed an interest in was working large parking lots. I knew that when I returned home, there would be times when the bus might have to drop me off at the outside edges of parking lots, and I wanted to know all I could about working such an area before I went home with Campbell.

One of the places Drew chose to take us to work on this was the mall. Because I was kind of uncomfortable in malls after my last experience, I protested at first, saying, "Well, I really don't do malls."

He put an end to that argument by saying, "Gee, it seems to me that your story of inspiration was the fact that a long-time grad, Phyllis Stevens, left you eating her dust in a mall!"

I couldn't say anything back to that, so to the mall Drew, Devin, and I went. I must confess, though, that since Drew got me with that reminder of my story of inspiration, I seriously considered tripping him in front of a delivery truck.

Once there, I was kind of excited, but mostly nervous. I

remembered what it had felt like to be lost in that big mall back in Johnson City. I figured that the malls in New Jersey must be way bigger than that one, so it really was a little frightening for me. As always, Drew encouraged me to not be afraid, but to take a chance on it. I was not all that sure about it, though.

As we walked through the large parking lot, Drew instructed Devin and me on how best to handle our dogs as we worked our way through the lot and to the door. A couple of times, due to drivers quickly backing out of parking places, Campbell gave me a good traffic check. Although this was a great learning experience, I was a wreck by the time we were done. In addition, I'd left my jacket in the van, so by the time we reached the door to the mall's food court, I was shivering from the cold and an attack of nerves.

I asked if it would be okay for me to sit and drink a cup of coffee so I could warm up and let Devin go first. Drew asked Devin what he thought; Devin didn't at all mind going first. So after Drew got me some coffee, he, Devin, and Gavin, Devin's dog, started out of the food court, leaving me to sit and drink my coffee in peace. I sat resting and listening to the people around me. Just from the way it sounded, I knew that the food court was huge, so I figured the mall would be way big and really, really crowded. This made me even more nervous. I tried to remember that Drew had never let anything happen to me and told myself I'd be okay if I just listened to him and did what I was told.

***

Finally they were back, and it was time for me to take my turn. As we left the food court, Drew began to describe things to me, as usual. I think that was one of my favorite things about working with him. He could always make word pictures of what we were encountering. I enjoyed that so very much.

Just as we were going through the doorway of the food

court and out into the mall, he mentioned that Campbell had walked right over a big piece of chicken on a toothpick, and that he hadn't even looked at it. Drew encouraged me to praise him. I did. Praising the dog when appropriate was another thing that everyone on the team always encouraged me and all the other students to do. It was always being repeated—in lectures, on trips, everywhere and by everyone—that if the dog liked what he was doing, he'd do a better job of it. I agreed, and so always tried to make sure Campbell knew I was pleased with his work.

As we went out into the mall, Drew asked, "What in malls do you enjoy looking at?" That was another thing I liked about working with him; he always tried to make what we were doing as enjoyable as it could be, even though training was a serious business. That seemed to be his way of trying to relieve us of some of the stress we were under while in class. I thought for a minute and then told him I really didn't know. I explained that I hadn't done much in malls over the last few years because I was a cane traveler, and unless I had someone to go with, I didn't do well in the mall.

I also told him, rather shyly, that even though I had no proof one way or another, I kind of felt that people avoided taking me along to the mall because it could be inconvenient for them. "I mean, look what happened when I went with Phyllis," I said. "Even that was kind of a disaster."

"Okay," he said, "let's go teach you how to make it so that's not the case anymore. There's no reason you shouldn't learn to keep up with anyone in a mall, whether they're sighted or blind."

Campbell and I followed Drew through the mall, and he described what we were passing. After a while, we began to encounter small sets of stairs in what I considered to be odd areas. Every time we'd encounter one of those sets of stairs, even though Campbell never failed to stop at the top of them, I would become nervous again.

After a while, I said, "I guess you've figured out by now that I don't like high places, and that I'm fearful that Campbell won't stop at the tops of stairs."

Drew laughed and looked up at me from where he stood in front of me, going down one of those sets of stairs. "I'd have had no idea if you hadn't told me," he said. "Come on, lady, let's get you over it!"

However, after we had maneuvered a few more sets of stairs, he began to let me take the ramps up and down. He said he wanted me to feel the joy of actually letting my dog work, letting him stretch it out a bit and put some speed in our step. I began to loosen up somewhat. It was amazing to me how Campbell's pull changed.

As we sped up, I called out to Drew, "Wow! I never knew I could walk through a mall like this!"

He looked back at me. "You like that?"

I laughed. "Yeah, cool! Awesome!"

He laughed and said, "Come on, lady! Hup that dog up!"

As Campbell and I began to relax into each other, our speed increased even more, and I began to know the joy of walking with my dog on a whole new level. Drew and I began to talk a little about things I liked. It was fascinating to me to be walking along behind him and carrying on a conversation while keeping up, not getting lost or running into people, and actually enjoying myself.

Soon we'd made our way to a statue shop, and as we were going inside, I said, "Wow! That was the most awesome time I ever had walking through a mall! I never knew it could be like that!"

Drew laughed. "Lots of benefits to having this furry pal by your side, huh?"

At that moment, I began to truly understand just what kinds of changes were about to take place in my life. I was actually going to become a more independent person.

As we spent a little time there, looking at different statues of dogs of all descriptions, I kept getting distracted by the thoughts of all the things I wanted to do with Donnie and Little D., things that we'd always avoided before because of my lack of mobility.

While we were there, Drew showed me a statue of a black Labrador that he described as being painted in living color. He explained that it was holding a ball in its mouth, and that even the tongue had been painted pink, exactly like a real dog's tongue. As I held that statue in my hands, running my fingers over every detail, listening to him describing it to me, I felt connected to it. I really wanted it a lot, but when Drew said it was time to get back to Devin and the food court, I gave it back. Letting him take it from me was somehow difficult. I've never been able to explain that, so I've never mentioned it until now.

As we left the store, I felt kind of down. I had very much wanted that statue, but the money my dad was sending me hadn't gotten there yet.

After we'd walked a little way away from the store, Drew stopped and asked, "What's up with the sad face?"

I suddenly felt childish and silly. I figured he wouldn't understand.

We stood there for a minute, and then he asked, "You really wanted that statue back there, didn't you?"

"Well," I said, "I do want it, but I'm not sure when the money my dad's sending me will be here, and I didn't bring what little money I had left with me."

Drew sighed. "I don't understand why you didn't bring any money to a mall."

"Well, I didn't know you'd let me go into places and shop!"

He laughed and squeezed my arm a little. "Why else would we go to a mall?"

I lowered my head a little and said softly, "Um, well, I thought we'd just be working on the parking lot and the mall area itself. Most times when I've worked with mobility instructors, I never got to do anything quite like this."

Drew was smiling when he turned Campbell and me around. "Come on. I think I can spot you the money till we get back to the school."

I couldn't help it; I had to smile, too. "Really?" I asked, a little more excitedly than I'd meant to.

"Yes," he laughed, "really. But let's get back and get that statue and get done. We've got other things to do today."

Just then I remembered that we also had a Country Trip scheduled for later that day. I hated those and said, "Aw, Drew, do we have to do that today?"

By the time we finished up in the statue shop and made our way back to Devin in the food court, we'd wasted so much time that there was no time for Country Work. So, as we got back in the van, Drew said, "Well, I'm gonna let you all off the hook today, and we'll do Country Work tomorrow." Devin didn't seem to care, but I would have hugged Drew's neck if I'd been able to get away with it.

***

Later that evening at supper, Drew and I met up, and I paid him for the statue. He tried to talk me into waiting for my other money to come, but I didn't want to. I was afraid that something would happen and I wouldn't end up having the money to pay him. I didn't want to end up having to leave still owing him money. Finally he relented and took the $25 for the statue. He asked me where I had put the statue. I told him it was sitting on my dresser, and that it would stay there till I got ready to go home.

The next morning, Drew came down to my room after breakfast to talk to me a little about the last part of my training. He told me that we needed to do more Country Work, and that we needed to do a session out someplace with Clicker Training.

Then he asked, "Have you made up your mind about going to New York?" Going to New York was optional. They encouraged it because working your dog in New York would really increase your confidence. I'd had doubts about going, because so many things frightened me, but he continued to encourage me daily to choose to go.

On this particular morning, as he was walking out my door, he said, "If you decide to go, I'll take you by yourself, just you and me. I think you'll enjoy it more that way. You'll know for sure that I'm with you, and maybe you'll feel safer about it."

I smiled and said, "Well, now, with an offer like that from such a big strong Yankee, I reckon a small-town Southern girl's just gonna have to accept."

He laughed and said, "I think you'll be glad you did, but you're really going to have to work on how you talk before you go, or else they're not going to like you." Then he started to walk away. I grabbed a scrap of paper off the desk, wadded it up, and tossed it at him. Amazingly, it hit him. He turned around and said, "Hey, lady, what's the big idea?" Then we were both laughing. He threw the paper wad back at me, and I actually caught the stupid thing. We had a paper wad fight for a minute, and then he was gone.

I stood smiling after him with Campbell by my side, wondering what it would be like to be around people that liked to laugh and have fun most of the time, people who didn't laugh at me for having dreams, people who actually believed in me and thought I was worth having around. And the thing I liked most? I was beginning to no longer be afraid of making mistakes. No one yelled at me if I spilled a drink. No one got upset with me if I forgot where I put something and needed visual assistance to find it. Those negative reactions were the norm in my daily life back home.

I remember one day when I was out on the patio at the

school having a smoke. The wind had been blowing, and the ashtray on the little table had turned over and spilled cigarette butts all over. I'd just passed Drew in the hall as he'd been cleaning up a mess someone's dog had made, and I was dreading going back inside to tell him about this additional mess. I didn't want to leave it because I was afraid some dog would eat the butts and get sick, but I was frightened to go inside and tell him. Although I didn't think he'd hit me, I was still afraid he'd yell at me and be angry.

I went in and got his attention. When he turned off the carpet shampooer, he said, "My ears are gonna ring the rest of the night." He turned around and saw my face.

"What's wrong, Patty?"

I hesitated. "Well, I turned over an ashtray outside, and there's a big mess out there. I don't want to leave it there, but I can't find it all to get it up." At that moment, I honestly thought I might cry. I hated making a mess like that; it always pissed Donnie off so much. But Drew's reaction was entirely different.

"Aw, I bet it's not that bad. Let me look." He walked out and in just a minute or two was back inside. "It wasn't that bad. No big deal. It's all cleaned up now. No worries, pretty lady."

I simply hadn't expected that reaction at all.

He tapped me on the arm. "You okay, honey?"

"Yeah. Just thinking, I guess. Thanks, dude."

"No problem," he said, and went back to cleaning the carpet after Campbell and I passed.

It was so nice to not have to feel as though I needed to be on guard all the time about what I said or did. It was wonderful to not have someone putting me down all the time, making me feel small and stupid. I felt accepted there, and even though I knew it was the most unrealistic thing on earth, I wished for just a brief moment that I would never have to go home. I even went to the technology center later in the day and spent some time online looking at housing and cost of living in the area. Knowing that I had very little education and just a few years of experience in anything other than factory work, I figured it was out of the question for me to even think of trying to step up a notch in my life. But it was something I wanted badly at that moment, and that I hoped to have someday.

Chapter 9

Training

Before I went to New York, there were things I had to learn. One of the newer training techniques was Clicker Training. I'd seen a few articles about it, but I really knew nothing much at all about how it worked or what its purpose was. Even though this was optional, I learned a long time ago that it's much better to know a thing and not need it than to need it and not know it. So I decided to attend the lecture and then decide if this was something I would want to take part in or not.

Lukas, one of the instructors, gave a lecture on Clicker Training and what it entailed. After hearing his talk, I decided that I might as well learn it. It seemed to me that it might be good to know if you found yourself in a situation where you needed to be able to find a specific place. So I signed up and waited to see what it was all about.

Later on that week, Drew and Lukas met me in my room one evening to begin the training. Lukas showed me the clicker and the target. He explained that you would attach the target to whatever item you wanted to teach your dog to find, like your regular ATM or a bus stop you were having trouble finding. Each time your dog rang the bell on the target, you immediately clicked the clicker. If you and your dog clicked and targeted at the same time, the dog got a treat. To me, that was a bit bothersome. I wondered what would happen if you should find yourself without treats.

When I asked, Lukas explained that once the dog had learned to target the item correctly every time you walked up to it, you would no longer use the clicker, so there would no longer be a need for a treat. He also explained that while you'd treat your dog while training, you'd also enthusiastically praise your dog, and that by the time you were through teaching it what you wanted it to find on a regular basis, praise would be more than enough.

And so we began.

We started out with Campbell just targeting the door in my room; I had to get in sync with him. I would first stand in front of the target, and when Campbell would be just about ready to put his nose on it, Lukas or Drew would tell me to get ready. Then when Campbell would target and ring the bell, I had to be very quick and click the clicker at the exact same time. If successful, Campbell would then get a piece of kibble. Next, we had to practice positioning ourselves farther and farther away from the target; each time, we would walk back up to it and have him target and me click at the correct time. Pretty soon we were getting the hang of it. Drew and Lukas told me we'd practice in other parts of the building, and that eventually we'd go out someplace and learn to target that, as well.

***

Another part of training, one that I thought was much more important, was traffic work. A guide dog is taught to do what's called intelligent disobedience when working in traffic. That's when you're standing at the street corner ready to cross, you've made your decision to go, you've given the dog the forward command, and the dog refuses to obey. If the dog refuses to obey, it means that there is still unsafe traffic or some sort of obstacle, and you have to see what it is that your dog is trying to get you to avoid. In the case of working traffic, nine times out of

10, it's traffic passing in front of you that will cause the dog to disobey.

To learn this, we had what were called traffic checks. With traffic checks, a trainer drives a car across in front of you while you're trying to cross a street, to see if the dog will stop as it's supposed to. Campbell did this very well. Even when they used one of those electric cars that hardly make any noise, Campbell did very well. Sometimes the car would be there cutting in front of you as you stepped off the curb. Sometimes the car would wait and cut in front of you after you were in the middle of the street. This part was extremely stressful to me, because you never knew which it would be or when it would happen.

When we first started to learn this, they would tell us when we were going to get traffic checks. But once we started getting used to the dogs stopping us abruptly, we just never knew when or exactly where the traffic checks were going to come. It made me nervous at first, because I was somehow frightened that Campbell wouldn't stop. Drew immediately noticed my hesitation at street crossings. He reassured me that Campbell had been taught very well to respect the car, and that he would stop me if and when I needed him to. As usual, Drew was right.

There was one time, however, when I had real trouble with traffic work; I remember the incident very clearly. One afternoon, we were walking to a statue shop to get statues of our dog's breed made; the statues would have on them the date on which each of us got our dog. It was my turn to cross the street. It was nothing more than a wide T intersection, so it should have been a straight shot across. But somehow, when it was my turn to go, I stepped off the curb, turned slightly to my left without realizing it, and got going in the wrong direction, starting out into the oncoming traffic.

Campbell was trying with all his might to push me back in line, but I didn't realize what he was doing, and instead of listening to him and going with him, I argued with him and tried to direct him in what I thought was the correct direction. Drew was standing on the curb talking with another student when he saw I'd strayed too far to my left. He yelled to me to go with my dog, but I didn't really hear him and kept going the way I had been. Drew yelled to me again, in a much more urgent tone, "Patty! Turn your body to the right *right now*! And follow your dog!"

Finally I realized what he wanted and where I was headed and quickly corrected. I barely made it before the light changed again. When he and the other student got across the street, I was standing on the curb, trembling and near tears. Drew came up to me, placed his hand on my shoulder, and asked if I was okay. I told him I was and asked him what I'd done wrong. He explained that when I'd stepped off the curb, I'd been turned just slightly to my left, and that slight incorrect turn had caused Campbell to read me wrong. So we'd started angling just a bit toward the oncoming traffic. He also explained that when Campbell had realized it was unsafe, he had tried to push me back in the direction I needed to go.

Drew said, gently but firmly, "If you follow your dog, you'll be safe."

I was still a bit shaken up, so Drew gave me a minute to catch my breath—but only a minute. Pretty soon, we were off and going again. I guess Drew figured that the longer I stood and thought about what had just happened, I might start thinking about what *could* have happened.

When I went to bed that night, I cried myself to sleep with the memory of it; I dreamed of it that night and for several nights afterwards. It made me a bit afraid to think I'd done that, and I found myself wondering what I'd do if that happened to me at home when I was out alone. I had to push those thoughts from my mind, though, and learn even better how important it was to let my dog have a lot of the control over what we did and how we did it. I was getting better at that, but I wasn't quite there yet.

***

The next part of training that I had to complete was Country Work. When doing Country Work, you're walking in an area where there are no sidewalks. The dog must keep you safely at the edge of the road, and you must check from time to time with either your foot or your cane to see if you're where you need to be. If not, you have to give your dog the right commands and hand signals to make the dog take you back to the edge of the road, out of the way of traffic. I hated that kind of work the very most. I found it to be exhausting and very nerve-wracking. But I knew that I had to learn it, and so learn it I did.

Chapter 10

New York

Over the weekend, I tried to prepare for my trip to New York. We were to go at the beginning of the coming week, and I was quite nervous about it. I didn't really know why; I guess it was because I didn't know what to expect. Finally the day arrived for Drew and Campbell to—as Jeff put it—"take the country girl to the Big City." I tried to eat breakfast, but Drew kept coming by the table and picking on me. It was all in fun, but a tiny part of me thought about losing him in the crowd and running off to work in Central Park with the artists and the fortune tellers. (That may sound weird, but it's always been a fantasy of mine!)

Eventually breakfast was over, and I was out in the front waiting for Drew. I sat on a bench smoking and petting Campbell, who was sitting patiently at my feet with his head lying in my lap. I scratched him behind the ears and told him what a beautiful love bug he was.

He looked up at me and licked my chin, as if to say, "Come on, Mom, you're gonna have to get some new material; everyone knows I'm a beautiful love bug."

Drew came outside, and we were on our way. When we got in the van, he handed me a pack of snack cakes. "What's this for?" I asked.

He laughed and said, "Its chocolate. Stress food, darlin'."

I laughed, began to take the wrapping off, and bit into the

chocolate-covered cake.

Just as we were about to pull out, Jeff came up to the van. "So country girl's going to the Big City?"

I turned in his direction but didn't say anything.

"Drew, you'd best look out for her," Jeff said. "She's liable to run off with the first city slicker that talks to her."

I smiled, but didn't join in their conversation.

I guess Drew picked up on that, because once we were on the road, he asked, "So what's going on with you? You're awfully quiet."

I sat eating my cake for a minute and thought about what to say. I suddenly felt as though I might cry with frustration. Even after all that time, I didn't think Drew truly understood me, how I work.

I started off by saying, "Well, honestly, I'm a little afraid to go to New York."

"Why? I'm going to be right there with you. I promise not to leave you for a second, and I won't let anything happen to you. Understand?"

I told him I did understand, that it was simply an irrational fear, and the only thing for me to do was to face it.

He said quietly, "I really hope that you'll be glad you did."

There was just a tiny hint of reservation in his voice. I think he was slightly worried about my reaction to all the different kinds of stimulation. If there was one thing we'd all learned about me during training, it was that the more stimulation I was experiencing at one time, the harder it was for me to focus and remain connected to Campbell.

We arrived at the Port Authority, and Drew found a place to park. Once out of the car, we stood together for a minute, and Drew described the view from up top. We headed for the stairs and began to make our way down to the subway platform. Once we'd made it onto the platform, Drew began to describe our surroundings. He also described what would happen when the train pulled in. He described what it would feel like under my feet and what it would sound like. He even went so far as to describe the rush of air that we would feel from the train as it came up in front of us.

I suddenly felt overwhelmed by all that and stepped hesitantly back.

Drew took my arm and steadied me. "We'll just stand here through a couple of trains," he said, "and let you watch them, so you'll know what to expect. It's okay. You're in no danger, and I'm right here beside you."

He kept his voice low and calm, and that went a long way toward soothing my nerves. I stood on the platform with Campbell by my side and waited to see what would happen. As the first train approached and the platform began to vibrate, I felt a little frightened. I reached out and touched Drew's arm, just to reassure myself that he was still there.

When the train had unloaded, reloaded, and moved on, he asked me what I thought about that.

I sighed a huge sigh. "I'm not sure."

"Okay, we'll let another one come and go. Then we'll see how you feel."

Another train came rumbling in and stopped at the platform. Again, the same loud noise, the same sharp jolt, and the same swoosh of air. Then, as quickly as it had come, it was gone.

Finally, after the third train, Drew said, "Okay, I think I'm just going to take you sighted guide. I don't think you're going to be encountering these often. I'm going to do this so we don't stress you so badly that you can't enjoy your trip."

As we boarded the train, I saw how easy it actually was. I was grateful to Drew for handling it that way; it went a long way toward lessening my fears. When it came time for us to leave the train, I didn't bother to hold his arm. I simply worked Campbell out of the car and onto the platform. Hell, he had known what to do all along. Once again, the problem was with me, not him.

More and more, that seemed to me to be the case. I found that if I heeded the advice of Drew and others—which was "Follow your dog!"—instead of going about it my way, I did much better. It was becoming increasingly evident to me that I'd been quite the control freak in a lot of things, and King Campbell, as I'd taken to calling him by this time, was seeing to correcting that tendency quite well.

As we stepped out into the city, I immediately started listening to the sounds around me. We started walking, and Drew began to describe what was around us. As we approached our first street crossing, he asked me to listen to the traffic and tell him what I heard. I stood quietly for a minute or two and then said, "The traffic sounds different."

There was a smile in his voice when he answered. "That's very good; there's more traffic in the city. That makes it move more slowly, which makes it quieter. Don't be deceived by that. When you begin to cross, your object is still the same: Get across the street as quickly and safely as you possibly can."

We walked down several streets. I remember crossing Fifth Avenue, and I also remember being amazed at how many people were standing at each crosswalk. Drew saw that I was paying attention to the people around me and quickly cautioned me not to do that.

"Don't pay attention to the people in order to see when it's time to cross. *They* might not be paying attention. You need to use your own skill, here. You need to depend on what you've learned to get you across the street, no matter who you're crossing with."

Eventually, we began to discuss where to eat lunch. Drew asked me what I liked to eat, and I mentioned that I liked Mexican food. So he took me to a great little Mexican place. The name of the place, of all things, was Chevys.

I had to laugh. "A Mexican restaurant called Chevys?"

Drew laughed, too. "You wait! It's really good. You'll like it."

When we got there, I was more than ready for a break. We settled down at our table and began to look at the menu. Finally we were ready to order, and then sat talking while we waited for our food.

As we enjoyed our lunch together, we talked about all sorts of things. Of course I had more guide dog–related questions, but soon our conversation turned to other topics, and we began to talk about things we liked to do and things we'd done. I even shared a bit more about my life with him. I told him how Donnie and I had gotten our start.

I asked a lot of questions that day, but one of the things I asked Drew was how he had been so sure that Campbell and I would be a good match. He was hesitant to answer that question at first, and he gave me a lot of instructor mumbo jumbo. I wasn't satisfied with that, so I pushed him a little harder. He ended up telling me a funny story.

"Well, the Sunday before we handed out dogs, I walked past your room, and you had your door open. You'd fallen asleep on your bed while reading a book. You were lying flat on your back with one foot propped on the footboard and one leg stretched off to the side. Your arms were spread open over your head, and it occurred to me that at that moment, you looked an awful lot like Campbell when he takes a nap."

I laughed. "Surely that wasn't what led you to your decision, was it?"

He was laughing, too. "Well, no, but that was part of it for sure."

He never really gave me any more answers about that subject, so I just let it drop.

Before we completely changed the subject, though, Drew asked, "You're not having any doubts, are you?"

I looked up quickly from my plate. "NO! Not at all! He's mine forever!" Almost unconsciously, I reached down, took

Campbell's leash from under my leg, and held it tightly in my hand.

Drew softened his voice and said, "That's right; he's yours forever." Then he reached across the table and laid his hand over the hand holding the leash. "Sweetheart, no one's going to take him from you. You're literally days from finishing your training and going home. That's your dog; you've earned him."

I thought for just a minute that I'd start crying right there, sitting at the table. But just at that moment, the server came back and asked if we needed anything. I was able to catch my breath as Drew settled the bill. I sat petting Campbell; he nuzzled my hand and gave me a kiss. This made me feel way better, so by the time we were ready to take off again, I was back to my reasonably calm self.

When we got outside, Drew told me we were going to walk all the way back to the Port Authority and not ride the subway at all. I was okay with that. I loved working Campbell any time I could, and it was very interesting to me to pass the different shops and things along the way.

Once again, Drew was describing things to me, and I began to get really caught up in the atmosphere of the city itself. It seemed to me that it was alive. It wasn't just because of all the people; it was the whole place. It just seemed to have a sort of thrum about it; you could literally feel the energy and vibration of the place in the air. It was all positive for me—or almost. Yes, I could feel a bit of underlying negativity from some of the people passing us on the sidewalk, but for the most part, I could only feel the excitement in the air around me.

As we walked, I felt a hand touching me to my right. All of a sudden, Drew was walking somewhat behind me, between me and the person to my right. He said, "No! Don't touch them!"

The woman next to me didn't seem to speak much English, if any, and again she reached out to touch us. I never did understand what she wanted, unless it was to get Campbell and me away from her. But as she reached for us again, Drew again stepped slightly in between us, and said in a firmer voice than before, "No! Don't touch them!" He had to say it a third time before she stopped.

Somehow or other, I got tickled by this. When we got to the next street crossing, and we were standing there waiting for it to be our turn to cross, I was laughing. Drew asked me what was so funny, and I just couldn't help myself. I said, "I couldn't help feeling like one of the Bible characters with leprosy, and I could hear you in my head saying, "Unclean, unclean! NO! Don't touch them! Unclean!"

A few of the people around us began to laugh, too, and Drew simply said in his best instructor's voice, "It's your light. Walk!" I laughed all the way across that street and quite a way down toward the end of the next block.

Sometimes while we were walking, I would become extremely focused on Campbell and myself, on the feeling that there were just the two of us. That is, for a few minutes at a time, it would seem to me that there was no one else there, only he and I. It would also seem to me that I no longer felt Drew's presence behind me.

Once, I started to turn around and say something to him about this, but Campbell and I were having such fun working together that I forgot it as quickly as I thought it.

When we reached the next intersection, I said to Drew, "For just a few minutes, there, it didn't even feel like you were behind me."

He answered, "If I ain't saying nothing, it means you're doing a good job."

I thought nothing more about it, and we began to make our way back up to where we'd left the van.

Later, I would learn from Drew that when I'd had that feeling of his not being behind me, it was because he'd gotten slightly distracted and had fallen just a bit behind me in the crowd, and for just a moment or two, he had lost sight of us. On the one hand, I was very glad he had decided not to tell me that while we were there in New York. On the other hand, I was darned proud of the fact that I'd felt so comfortable with Campbell during those moments that I'd ended up simply pushing away the thought that it didn't feel like Drew was there and had continued on down the street with my dog. I didn't like to think about what my reaction might have been had I turned around and realized Drew was not right there. It probably would have caused me to have a panic attack. But once again, Drew had known the correct way to handle the situation, exactly the right thing to say to me, and so the experience I had that day was fantastic.

Once back up on the top of the parking area, Drew and I stopped for a moment. He turned to me, and as we faced each other, he asked, "So, what did you think about your first trip to New York, young lady?"

I stood for a moment, thinking about the day's events and listening to the sounds of the city around me.

He gently touched my arm. "Hello? Earth to young lady!"

I laughed, a bit embarrassed. "I liked it very much, and I can't think of a better person to have gone with for my first time." We stood for a moment or two. Again, I was lost in my own private, happy thoughts. How long we stayed like that, I'm not really sure. It had been a good day for me, and I hoped for Drew as well.

***

On the way back to the school, we talked about a lot of neat stuff. We talked about music, and Drew played me a couple of songs from a CD he had with him that he really liked. He left me listening to it while he stopped to run an errand. He seemed to listen to mainly country music, and for the most part, that's just not my thing. But some of the music he listened to was pretty good, so I never had any trouble enjoying anything he played. I even remember asking him about borrowing a couple of the CDs he had so I could burn them to my computer, but we never got around to that.

After he got back in the car from his stop, as we continued the trip back to the school, somehow our conversation turned once again to my other disabilities, mainly my bipolar disorder. I think that topic came up because I asked him to remind me to take my afternoon dose of medications when we got back. He asked me a little more about what those medications did for me, and I tried again to explain to him about bipolar and what it can cause a person to do.

While I do believe that he was paying attention and listening, I don't think he ever truly understood. That's a problem for a lot of people, and I never hold it against them. It's very hard for someone to comprehend this type of thing if they have never experienced it themselves or if they have never lived around someone with the disorder. If you meet someone who suffers from bipolar but is very stable at the time, then if that person becomes sick later on, it can be extremely hard for some to deal with.

I have lost many people over the years to this disorder. For some, it was simply more than they were willing or able to deal with. It's not their fault; it's just what it is. It can be very hurtful to observers when someone is in the grip of an episode and has little to no control over what's happening to them. But again, I don't hold a lack of understanding against people. I believe that if I want people to be tolerant of me and my disabilities, I need to be tolerant of them and their problems or weaknesses as well.

When we returned to the school, I stopped just before going inside.

"Drew?"

He turned and faced me.

"Yes?"

I stood for a moment, not at all sure how to say what I felt. Then I found the words.

"Thanks for being you and the kind of instructor you are."

Before he could answer, I turned, said "Inside!" to Campbell, went through the door, and was gone. I've always felt that he would have said something if I had given him the chance, but to this day, I don't know what it would have been. It probably would have been nothing more than a simple thank you, but since I didn't stay to find out, I'll never know.

It's that kind of thing right there that can, if allowed, be the beginning of a problem. I remind you again, fellow grads: Don't ever mistake someone's kindness and professionalism for anything more. It's not fair to you, and for sure, it's not fair to them.

To you, the staff, I say: If you think someone's confused about what they feel, don't ignore them. That's not always the best way, and under certain circumstances, it can in fact make the problem worse.

For all concerned, it's always best to simply speak up and say what you think and feel. If you're going to have to hurt someone, it's better to do it quickly rather than to allow a situation to continue until it becomes highly inappropriate and out of control.

Looking back at the circumstances I found myself in, both during my training and after I went home, I see now just how easy it was for me to get all mixed up about a lot of things. That's one of the reasons I'm writing this book. I'm hopeful that my writing about these experiences will enable those who shared them with me and who are reading about them now will understand things a bit better than before. I also hope that my book can help others who find themselves in similar circumstances.

I don't regret that trip to New York or anything else that happened during my time at The Seeing Eye. It was an experience that will live forever for me. Do I expect Drew and the others on my team to remember half of what I write about in these pages? No, I don't. Do I hope that if and when he and others read this, they might remember at least some of these things and enjoy them, maybe have a laugh or two over them? Yes, I do, very much. I also hope that it helps to clear things up a bit more for all concerned.

Chapter 11

Getting the Hang of It

As the end of class drew closer, I began to feel more and more comfortable working Campbell. I will never forget the first time I went somewhere without even really thinking about it. We'd just come out of a mid-morning lecture, and it was almost lunchtime. Somehow I'd gotten it into my head that it was lunchtime, and so Campbell and I quickly made our way out of the upstairs common lounge and down the main stairway to the first floor and the main hall. I was feeling hungry and thinking it was already time for me to be in the dining room, so instead of heading back to my room as usual, I headed down the main hallway at top speed.

When I entered the dining room, it seemed to me that there were more people than usual in there. But I just figured that maybe they'd done a tour that day and that there were more guests than usual at lunch. As Campbell led me through the crowded room to my chair, I was amazed at how well he did. We didn't run into one person, and we went straight to my table and then to my chair without a single mistake. I was so proud of him that I knelt down right there on the floor and hugged him to me, telling him over and over what a wonderful dog he was and how much I loved him. In turn, he looked up at me while wagging his tail furiously, pounding it very noisily on the table, and licked my entire face with two good swipes of his big tongue.

Just then one of the servers walked up and said, "Hi, Patty.

You're early today!"

Suddenly I realized that I'd come while the dining room was still full of staff having their lunch. I stood quickly and said, "Oh, I'm sorry! I guess I'd best get out of here!"

She told me I could stay, but I was afraid of getting into trouble, so I turned quickly, and just as easily as Campbell had worked through that crowd of people coming in, he went right back out again.

As we left the dining room, I found Jeff standing there at the door. "Hungry today?" he asked.

I laughed and said, "I guess so. I had no idea I was so early. If you saw me, why didn't you stop me?"

He laughed and said, "No way! I wouldn't have stopped you for anything. That's the best work I've seen you do yet. You guys flew in here like you'd been doing it all your lives, and I wouldn't have missed that for anything."

Suddenly it mattered not one bit to me that I had walked through all that staff when I wasn't supposed to be there. I was so proud of Campbell and myself for the good and quick work that I simply went right back down the hall and on down to the smoking patio to reward myself with a smoke and Campbell with a good ear-scratching. As I sat in the sun, waiting for the call for lunch to really come, I smiled to myself and thought, "Hmm! I might just make a guide dog handler yet." It was one of the very best moments of my whole time at the school.

I know it might seem simple to some, but for me to feel so sure of myself that I hadn't even stopped to wonder why there wasn't an instructor at the door directing student and dog traffic meant that I really was starting to get the hang of what I was doing. I realized that I liked the feeling quite a lot.

When the call for lunch finally came, I got up and said to Campbell, "All right, Love Bug, let's do it again." We took off. Right back to the dining room we went, then right back to our table, just as before.

Campbell's Rambles

As I was sitting having lunch with my friends, Drew came up and said, "I hear you and Campbell tried to crash early lunch today!"

I laughed and said, "Guess we got carried away."

"I'm very glad," he answered. "It's good to see that you're starting to feel better about this."

I sat for a minute and then said, "It sure beats trying to get through a crowd like that using a cane. If I'd been coming through all those people with a cane, I'd never have gotten it done. For sure, my cane would have gotten tangled up with someone's feet or chair legs or something. But with Campbell, there might as well not have been any people in here. Pretty cool, if you ask me!"

He was smiling as he said, "Well, looks like we've taken the redneck from Tennessee and turned her into a redneck guide dog handler at last."

He walked away, and I hoped he felt at least half as happy and satisfied about it at that moment as I did.

I've done a lot of neat things with Campbell since then, but I won't ever forget that, because it was the very first time I felt completely together and as though I might actually know what I was doing. I knew one thing for sure: I never wanted to have to depend on a red and white folding cane again if I could help it. As if he could read my mind, Campbell put his paw on my leg and began to lick me, as if to say, "You don't need any stinking stick as long as you have me!"

89

Chapter 12

Last Trip

As the final week of training began, Drew told Devin and me that we were going to go to the South Street Creamery for our last trip together. Drew's other two students had been retrains and had already gone home, so it would just be the five of us: Drew, Devin, Gavin, Campbell, and me. However, I didn't want to go.

When I told Drew that, he threatened to take me to the hospital. "I don't believe it!" he said. "You don't want to go get ice cream? Should I call an ambulance?"

I told him I was flat broke. I explained that I did have a little bit of money left, but that I needed to hold onto that for my trip home. I even went so far as to ask him if we could go someplace else. Devin had said he didn't mind either way, just so long as we all got to do something together before we left. Drew, however, would not relent. He was going to that darned Creamery or bust.

When the day for us to go arrived, we were in the dining room having lunch. When they came around to ask if we wanted dessert, I went ahead and got one. I figured that if I couldn't have ice cream at the Creamery, I'd have it there with my cake.

Just as I got ready to take my first bite, Drew walked up and asked, "What are you doing? Now we can't eat ice cream!"

I just looked at him. "Well, I can't have any from there, anyhow. I don't have any more money."

He walked away without another word. I went back to my

dessert, grumbling again about not wanting to go.

When it was time for our trip, I wasn't in a great mood at all. I went willingly enough to the van, but I didn't participate in Devin and Drew's conversation unless one of them spoke to me directly. When we got there, Drew parked the van a little distance away and had us walk the rest of the way. Again, I was not very happy about being there, so I was the last one out of the van.

Drew seemed to be getting a little annoyed with me. "Come on!" he said. "Out of the van. And stop pouting."

That just about did it for me, so I was nearly in tears as I followed Devin and Drew. It wasn't so much that I was upset about where we were; I guess it was just kind of the breaking point for me. We were almost done with training, and it can be very emotional there at the end. It's terrifying and exciting all at the same time to think of going home with your dog and being on your own in a strange new world.

By the time we got to the Creamery, though, I was feeling a little better. Working Campbell did then, and still does today, have that effect on me; it always cheers me up. So by the time we made it to the door, at least I wasn't growling at Drew anymore. Besides, it never went well for me when I copped an attitude with him. It never failed to put me on the losing end of things.

Once inside, we found a table, and Devin and I settled our dogs underneath.

Drew sat down beside me and asked, "What kind of ice cream do you want?"

I turned to him, stuck my tongue out at him, and said, "Really?" That was all.

Drew chuckled to himself and then talked to Devin a minute about what he wanted. They exchanged money and Drew walked away.

Devin said, "Come on, Patty, cheer up! It's almost time to go home. We made it, you know?"

I sighed, "I know, but being in here without eating ice cream—that's no good."

Just then, Drew walked back to the table and handed Devin what he'd asked for. Then he turned to me and said, "Here's enough chocolate ice cream to bounce you to the moon. Sure am glad I'm not on night duty!" He set a bowl of ice cream in front of me that had at least two or three different kinds of ice cream in it—big, big scoops of it, too, all with chocolate of some sort. He knew how much I loved chocolate ice cream and had gotten me some. I think Devin may have helped him with it, but I didn't ask.

I just looked up at Drew with tears in my eyes and said, "Thanks! You didn't have to do that."

Drew laughed and handed me a tissue. "I cannot win with you, lady. You cry when you're upset and you cry when you're happy. I think I've used more tissues with you than with any other student I've ever worked with. Eat your ice cream."

I dug into it, feeling better than I had all day. Only trouble was, I'd also eaten that darned dessert at school, so by the end of the bowl, I was starting to feel just a bit sugared out. But I wouldn't have left one drop of ice cream in that bowl if you'd paid me.

Once I was done with my ice cream, I asked, "Do you think I could get a glass of ice water?"

Drew looked up and said, "Sure, if you can go get it." The place was packed, and for just a minute, I thought about forgetting about it, but then I thought to myself, That's dumb. If you can't walk to the counter from right here and ask for a glass of water, how the hell do you intend to go home with this dog?

I got up and got my bearings, then walked away from the table. Once I was in line, I waited for my turn. Twice someone asked to pet Campbell, and twice I sent them away with a firm but polite no. I was getting a little annoyed, because it was the same person who asked twice, but I tried to remain polite about it.

Finally I had my water and was ready to go back to the table. Suddenly I wasn't exactly sure where it was in that large room filled with people and noise. I called out to Drew and said, "Hey, Drew, make some noise!"

He said, "Crickets! Crickets! Crickets!"

I walked up to the table and sat down with my water.

"Drew?"

"What?"

"Do you rub your legs together when you make that noise?"

Devin got tickled by that, and the mood lightened even more. We sat together for a while, talking and laughing. As we talked, Devin and I asked some questions. We wanted to know what kinds of stuff Drew wrote in his reports about us. Drew talked to us about the different things he had to include, and when I asked him what he wrote about me, he said, "That you need to believe more in yourself."

He talked to me about that a little. He encouraged me to start believing in myself more, to take chances sometimes, and to not always assume that I would screw up. I was starting to get to where I felt that I could do more of that, but I never did feel that Drew really understood why I was the way I was. But how could he? Of course no one knew how things were for me at times. And how could they? Can any of us ever know exactly how another person feels, or why?

When we got ready to leave, I was a lot happier than when I'd arrived. As Campbell and I started toward the door, we passed Drew. I stopped and said, "Thanks, dude; I appreciate it."

"You're very welcome. You couldn't come to the Creamery without eating ice cream, could you?"

I didn't say anything more; I figured it was best left alone.

As we started walking to the van, I suddenly felt a bit disoriented. I couldn't decide exactly where the van was in the parking lot, so I stood for a minute, not sure of what to tell Campbell. Campbell, however, was tugging at me to come on, but I wouldn't go with him.

Drew was standing a little ahead of me, and he called out to me, "Come on, lady! Take a chance. There's a 50 percent chance you'll be right."

I told Campbell "Forward!" and to the van we went, straight away.

"See, I told you," said Drew.

I climbed into the van, and we were off and running once again.

Once we got back to the school, Campbell and I were walking inside and Drew was behind us. I walked right up to the door without any hesitation on the step. That had been a problem for me all along, so when we got to the door quickly and without any problem whatsoever, Drew called out to me, "Great job, lady, and handsome dog, too!"

I laughed. "Thanks!" I answered.

Then I went on my way to my room. It had turned out to be a pretty okay day after all.

Chapter 13

Readying Myself To Go Home

Finally it was the night before the big day. Lecture was over, we had our going-home packets with all our info in it, and we were running around getting all sorts of last-minute stuff done. Earlier in the day, I'd taken Campbell to meet with their vet, get his records, and learn all about him. He weighed 67 pounds and was 24 inches at the shoulder. He was as healthy as a horse. I was pleased to learn that the ear infection he'd been battling was cleared up and that all was well with my boy. I'd even had him microchipped, so that if he should ever get lost, I'd be able to find him more easily.

Now I was in my room, pacing back and forth with nerves. I had talked to Donnie earlier in the evening. There had been tornadoes all over the area there, and in fact, all across the U.S. It was April 27, 2011, and I had just a few more hours in the protection of what some called The Seeing Eye bubble. It had certainly been that. I couldn't have told you one thing that was going on in the rest of the world. I don't think I'd seen more news than a weather report since I'd been there; I'd pretty much done nothing but focus on training and what I had to learn. There had been so very much information that I still wrestled with the fear that I might get home and forget important things. Several times I'd forgotten commands or had gotten them mixed up. A couple of times, I'd confused poor Campbell until I thought he'd go and tell Drew, "I am not going home with this ass-backward human!"

One of the big problems I'd had all throughout class remained unresolved; I still had problems with my sense of direction. Sometimes I went left when I was supposed to turn right; I could get those mixed up even if someone was coaching me from behind. At that point, it had been and still was a huge source of stress and frustration to me. Before my training with Campbell, I had never realized that I had such a problem with distinguishing left from right. All along, Drew had been encouraging me to remember what hand the dog was in: "Left!" That helped, but it didn't cure me. One time, I tried saying *dog* in my head instead of left, but all that did was cause me to say "dog" out loud—which of course did nothing but confuse Campbell and make others around me either nervous or get tickled.

As I packed up my things and got together a load of dirty laundry to wash before leaving, I thought back to some things I'd done during class. All in all, training had been a wonderful—if grueling—experience. I had made a few really good friends, and I had learned things I never knew I would or could.

I had learned some things about myself, too, and some of them bothered me a bit. One of those was the realization that I wanted more out of my life at home than I had been getting. I hoped that having Campbell would make that possible.

Since I'd been there at the school, I'd begun to feel like a real person again—alive, and as though I really was somebody. I had begun to feel that maybe I was actually worth something. I had begun to believe that the snide, hurtful remarks that Donnie and others sometimes made when I talked about things in my past didn't matter anymore. They were very good at putting down many things that I had accomplished in my past—like moving out at the age of 17 and a half, learning a trade, and then earning and saving enough money to get my own place. Or when I was in the sixth grade and only 11 and a half years old, I had been put in the high school band. And the year I went into the ninth grade, I made first chair flute.

Now I was thinking, so what if I had lived in the dorm for six months while I trained and learned that job? I got it, didn't I? And didn't I move out all on my own and without any help from my parents—except that they brought some of my furniture and personal items to my new place, took me to the store, filled my fridge with food as a welcome home present, and encouraged me to be as independent as possible? Maybe, I thought, it's not me that Donnie and the others ought to be making remarks about!

As I put my clothes in the washer, I realized that I was kind of proud of myself and of who I was becoming. Maybe I *could* be a successful young lady, the kind of person Drew thought I could be. Maybe I didn't need to pretend I was a bad-ass redneck who had to walk around proving all the time that that was what she was. Maybe I had real potential, and maybe having Campbell would give me the courage and ability I needed to see just how far I could go.

I wasn't quite sure, but I was sure that I was gonna try.

Finally I was all done and packed, and Campbell was tired out from going up and down the stairs to the laundry room with me, so I called it a night. Everyone seemed to have disappeared, and since I didn't know exactly where the night instructor's room was, and there was no one on my floor to annoy, I decided I'd curl up with my book and fall asleep. I figured I wouldn't sleep very well or very long, but it turned out that I'd worked myself and Campbell pretty hard, so when I got him settled in his crate and myself into bed, it didn't take long to pass out.

As I drifted off, I whispered softly into the dark, "Thank God and Goddess, thanks to Drew, Campbell, and The Seeing Eye, for helping me get my life back." I was beginning to think that this might just be a new beginning for me. Had I known what awaited me, I might have turned and run. But I had no way of knowing, so I went forward with all my hopeful plans and dreams.

Chapter 14

My Last Morning

Early in the morning of April 28, 2011, I talked with Donnie on the phone. He told me that 20 people had been killed in my hometown and surrounding areas due to the storms they'd had the night before.

We also talked about things that would have to happen when I returned home with Campbell. I explained to him about how there couldn't be a lot of people at the house the first night home, and how Campbell would have to be on a leash with me or on a tie-out for the first two weeks. After that, I would then begin allowing him small amounts of freedom at a time. He would sleep in his crate at night.

Donnie did not seem to understand this even after I explained it to him as clearly as I could. He argued with me, saying that it all sounded a little harsh. He even made the statement, "Well, it's not like they'll know what you do when you get home, so it's not like you really have to do all that."

I tried to get him to understand, but I finally gave up and simply told him, "Donnie, it's not open for discussion." We decided to agree to disagree. I thought maybe he might get a better understanding after spending some time with us when we got home.

Somehow, though, it was beginning to be less and less important to me whether he understood or not. Something in me had changed while I was there at The Seeing Eye. At first I hadn't really understood what those changes were all about, but I was beginning to. I had begun to be treated with a lot of respect by those who were successful, educated, and intelligent people. It had made me begin to think that maybe I could have just a bit more out of my life than I was getting at the time. I realized that I had been allowing others to control me, to make decisions for me, even as to where I went, how I went there, and when.

I knew now that with Campbell by my side, I no longer had to depend on others to help me get to bus stops, stores, or places to eat if I didn't want to. I realized that I would be able to go many different places, now, quite successfully—and even with my friends, because I could walk along with them of my own free will and with little to no assistance from anyone. This went a long way toward making me feel better about myself, and I hoped that once I got home, I would have the courage to keep the new attitude I was adopting. I'd already learned that people who were serious about living a decent life weren't impressed with my bad-ass redneck attitude, and that they saw me as a woman who had much potential and could really make something of herself if only she'd believe in herself and try. So Donnie's attitude of "It's not like they'll know" bothered me a lot. To me, that was just underhanded and disrespectful.

As I packed the last of my own and Campbell's things, I felt nervous but excited. I knew that I was embarking on a new adventure, also that I had closed a chapter in my life and was beginning a new one. I truly felt reborn.

As I put things in the suitcase, Campbell followed me around the room, sniffing everything and wagging his tail furiously all the time. He wanted to help me pack—or, as it turned out, unpack. As soon as I put the things in, he wanted to take them out again. Finally, I had no choice but to put the big pest in his crate with his bone, in the hopes that he would chew himself to sleep for a while. But no way! He decided that if he

Campbell's Rambles

couldn't distract me by unpacking my suitcase, he would lie on his back in his crate, toss his bone up in the air, and let it make lots of noise banging around in his crate. When I told him to knock that off, he simply moaned a big moan and tossed it up in the air again.

I couldn't help but laugh. "Campbell, you really are just like your mother!" I knew in my heart that Campbell and I were going to make a successful team, and I was proud to pieces of what we'd already accomplished together. I just hoped that Drew and the rest of my team were proud of us, too.

Then I was done, and they were calling us to the common lounge for a small breakfast of fruit and pastries, along with coffee and juice. The four of us students who were left gathered in the lounge, talking and laughing with one another. We were all nervous and excited. I know that I, at least, had a little fear thrown in for good measure. Also, although I knew there wasn't anything to do for it, I felt a tiny bit sad that Drew wouldn't be driving me to the airport.

As we sat sharing our last meal together, we exchanged addresses, phone numbers, and email info. We wanted to stay in touch with one another if we could. I gave Devin my info and he gave me his.

I had even begun to make some plans for when I returned home. I'd had a hard time doing that earlier, because I had felt that Donnie and I were becoming disconnected somehow. Now I no longer worried about that. I had worked too hard and had come through too much to let that stop me. I wanted nothing but to be the very best guide dog handler I could be. I hoped that I would make Drew and the rest of The Seeing Eye proud; I hoped they'd know that their time, effort, and money hadn't been wasted on me. I wanted everyone to know what a fantastic place The Seeing Eye was: what it had done for me and what it could do for others. I had hopes that someday I would be able to do something worthwhile to repay them for their kindness to me.

Many people were responsible for the fact that at my feet was a beautiful black Labrador named Campbell Lee, a dog who had already become my very best friend, and who had already gone a long way toward literally saving my life. I had no idea of the things that were in store for me when I returned home. I had no way of knowing what changes were about to take place in my life, and I was in no way prepared for them. But the one thing I knew above all was that I could face anything as long as Campbell walked happily by my side.

As the morning drew to a close and we began to get ready to leave and go our separate ways, I reached down and gave Campbell a good scratching behind his ears and said, "Campbell Bug, it's time to begin our new life. Are you ready?" As if on command, he stood and positioned himself beside me. He snorted a happy snort, as if to say, "Sure, Mom! What took you so long to catch up?"

***

As I walked out of the common lounge into the hall, I had a serious attack of nerves. I suddenly couldn't remember what I was supposed to do next, and on top of that, I knew I was getting ready to come to the top of the stairs. Once again, my fear and panic set in. I literally couldn't breathe.

One of the instructors walked up to me and asked me what was wrong. I couldn't talk; I couldn't do anything but cry. I was so angry with myself for feeling this way, when just minutes before, I'd been thinking about all the changes I wanted to make in my life, changes I knew I could really make. What in the world was wrong with me?

Shannon walked me over to a chair at the side of the hall, sat me down, and knelt down to talk to me. As she took my hand in hers, she asked me again what was wrong. After a minute, I was able to tell her I had suddenly not remembered what to do next, and that once again, I had been overcome by that same old fear of the stairs. I felt so inadequate, suddenly, and as though maybe I really didn't know what I was doing after all. I also felt very frightened about returning home with Campbell, because something inside me kept saying, "You're going to end up alone; you're making a mistake." I couldn't understand any of my fears. They just didn't go along at all with what I had been thinking just before.

Suddenly Drew was at my other side. As he reached for my other hand, he asked me what was going on. Through my tears, I tried to explain to him, but he just kept telling me that I would be all right. When I told him I didn't want to go home alone, he gently smoothed my hair and said, "You're not alone. You have Donnie there waiting on you." I knew that was so, but that little nagging feeling inside me simply would not go away, and I didn't have the right words to convey to Drew what I felt. I knew that it wouldn't make any difference anyway; it wasn't as though I could stay there.

Eventually I began to calm down, and then I remembered that when I was packing earlier, I couldn't find Campbell's Kong toy. I looked up at Drew with tears in my eyes once again and said, "I can't find Campbell's Kong. He'll want it when we get home. I can't leave without it!"

Gently squeezing my hand, Drew said, "Now *that* I can do something about!"

He coached me down the stairs, and after looking around for a minute or two, he found the Kong under the bed. We put it and Campbell's bone in my backpack, and I sat down on my bed to catch my breath. Drew started out of the room, saying he'd be back in a minute. Just then, Sue walked in and told me she'd be taking me to the airport, and that it was almost time to go. Suddenly I wanted nothing more than to crawl back in my bed and hide, but I knew I couldn't do that.

Just then, Devin, his dog Gavin, and Drew came back in.

Drew said, "Devin wanted to say goodbye again." I stood up, and Devin and I hugged our goodbyes.

"Remember," Devin said, "you can do this. Just remember to breathe and enjoy yourself."

I hugged him tightly and asked, "Aren't you scared at all?"

He laughed, "Hell, yeah! But we can't go home and not try, not after all the hard work that we've all done to get here." I knew he was right, so I gathered my courage once again. Devin kissed my cheek and went out.

For just a moment, it was just Drew, Campbell, and me.

Drew walked over. "How about a hug for your old instructor?"

I reached out, put my arms around him, and hugged him tightly to me. He hugged me back. I was going to miss him terribly. I'd never felt so safe with anyone. As was the norm for me when hugging someone I wanted to remember well, I buried my face against his shoulder and breathed deeply of his scent. It was the scent of learning, trust, and safety. He'd done a lot for me that I will probably never be able to talk about. We'd had a lot of fun together during training, and I'd gained a whole new perspective on life, thanks to him. I didn't—and still don't today—think that the man has any idea how much he helped me.

As we separated, he brushed a couple of strands of hair from my face, and said softly, "You're going to do just fine. Don't be so afraid, and remember what I told you. Take a chance, because there's a 50 percent chance you'll be right."

For what I thought would be the last time, he took a tissue from his pack and wiped the tears from my face. At that moment, I wanted nothing more than to press a stop button. I suddenly had a whole list of questions I hadn't thought of until then. In addition, I had fears I'd been keeping secret. There were things I thought I might be able to say if I had just one more day, but now the time was gone. There were also the old fears:

Would he believe me if I told him my secrets? Would he care? Would he think that the things that were going on in my life that I wanted to tell him about were no big deal? Would he think that my fear of what might happen in the future was ridiculous, and that I was just exaggerating?

A jumble of thoughts and scenarios ran around and around in my head. How to begin? Was there any way to stop this from happening? Could I somehow avoid going back into things I knew now weren't at all right?

We stood for a moment not saying anything. Then, knowing there was simply nothing to do but go forward, I pushed all that out of my mind and said to him, "Now you get down there and give that dog a hug goodbye! I know you love him too, and that's okay." He hesitated, and I said, my voice cracking with emotion, "Yankee! Act like you've got some sense and tell that dog goodbye! You're not going to damage our bond by doing it, and you darn well know that!"

He laughed a little and knelt down to say goodbye to Campbell, saying, "Okay, take it easy!"

Campbell did exactly what I'd known he would do. He licked Drew's face all over, sliming him up right good. I laughed through my tears, and said, "It's slime time!" I knew he loved that dog.

Oh, don't get me wrong. I know those instructors get attached to all the dogs they train, but I could feel the special love between those two, and it didn't bother me one bit. I knew there were some grads who didn't like that sort of thing; however, I believe that they simply didn't understand it.

Drew stood and said, "Now, take care of yourself and stay out of jail. I'm not bailing your ass out if you end up in there. I'll rescue Campbell if I need to."

We both laughed, shared another brief but tight hug, and then he was gone. For just a few minutes, it was only Campbell and me there together, and I felt a bit sad. Then Sue was there, telling me it was time to go. So I gathered my things, took Campbell's harness in my hand, and said, "Forward, Campbell! Outside!" Then we were off, ready to begin our new lives together.

Editor's note: Go here to see what a Kong toy looks like: **http://www.petco.com/product/2324/KONG–Dog–Toy.aspx**

Part 3

The Journey Begins

Chapter 15

False Alarm

As Campbell and I entered the main lobby, several people came up to us to say goodbye. First there was Jeff, our class supervisor. He wished me a happy life with Campbell and told me we'd done a great job in class.

And once again, there was Lukas asking to pet my dog. He'd been doing that all through class as a way to get me and the others used to people coming up and asking to pet our dogs.

I smiled at him and said, "Sure, this time you can pet my dog!"

He gave Campbell a quick pat on the head and me a hug. He told me to behave myself and to enjoy the heck out of my dog.

As Sue, Campbell, and I made our way to the van along with one of the other instructors and her student, I felt a little disjointed again, but I pushed the feeling aside and kept going.

Once at the airport and through security, we sat and waited until it was time to board my plane. We chatted a bit about different things, and then they were calling my flight. The agent who was going to assist Campbell and me to the plane was there, and I was hugging Sue goodbye. As Campbell and I walked away, I called back to Sue over my shoulder, "You keep that Gibbon straight, and give him a kick in the ass for me every now and then, okay?" She laughed and assured me she would. Then Campbell and I were off.

Or so we thought.

111

Once we were on the plane and settled in our seat, I began to arrange my things for the trip to Charlotte, North Carolina. Then the fun began. For the next three hours, we made our way from one part of the runway to another. There were bad storms in the area, and our flight had been delayed. Finally the pilot made the announcement we'd all been dreading. Our flight had been canceled, and we were going back to the terminal. Eventually the flight attendant was there beside me, and Campbell and I were getting ready to leave the plane.

I began to get Campbell ready to move. I put his harness back on and got him into position—which, by the way, is no easy task when you have a tall Lab that weighs 67 pounds, and there is also very little room to move. I got him situated, and then I learned that we would not be using the jetway to exit the plane, because of other planes using it. They were bringing a large set of stairs. The stairs were put in place, and when it was time for Campbell and me to leave, I didn't think there would be any problem.

Boy, was I wrong! It turned out that these stairs were very high, and the platform at the top was grated and see-through.

Now, let's stop here, because I need to let you know that Campbell has been trained to avoid such things whenever possible. So when he saw what he was expected to cross to get to the stairs, he sat himself down in the doorway of the plane and said in his best doggie body language, "NO WAY! Ain't nothin' good gonna come from this!" I coaxed him and talked to him, but he would not budge.

One of the security guards suggested that I allow them to carry him off the plane. I refused. I told them that we might encounter this again someplace, and that I had to talk him down. I was also very worried about the possibility that Campbell might flip out from fear and jump from the guard's arms. A fall like that could hurt him badly enough to remove him from service before he ever began. That was something I absolutely could not risk.

Now remember that I myself had a healthy fear of heights, and it turns out that these stairs were possibly as much as 25 feet off the ground. Neither Campbell nor I was very happy about our situation, but I tossed my fear of heights aside and turned myself around, so that my back was to the stairs. I asked the security staff to spot me and let me know when I'd almost reached the first step. The wind was blowing hard and the stairs were shaking. Campbell was shivering and I was terrified, but I couldn't show any of my own fear to him. I knew that it was very important for me to handle this situation exactly right, because what I did at that time would affect us as a team for the rest of our lives together.

I began to back up, squatting down and talking softly to Campbell. He was crouched down and did not want to move. He was making a soft whimpering noise. I began to pull him and continued talking very calmly and softly to him. He was as scared as I was, and it was obvious that he didn't want to do it, but he came slowly across with me. I can't imagine what must have been going through his mind. But I *can* imagine how happy he would have been to see Drew appear at that moment. Come to think of it, it wouldn't have hurt my feelings any, either, but we were on our own.

What I didn't know then was that it was the first of many times that we would be afraid and on our own.

When I reached the steps, I stood and turned myself around, and Campbell fell into position beside me. I petted and praised him up and down. He'd done a fabulous job of obeying me, and it no longer mattered to me how frightened he and I had been just moments before. What mattered was that we had done it.

I asked him if he was ready. He kind of shook himself and lined up right with me. I picked up the harness handle and proudly walked down that flight of stairs with my dog. At the bottom, I knelt down and put my arms around his neck, telling him what a very good boy he was. The flight attendant was in tears. I was in tears. I hugged him tightly and buried my face deep in his fur. As I took a deep breath and filed away the memory of his smell, he nuzzled my neck with his nose. That was the smell of trust, of love. It's a smell I hope I will never, ever forget.

Suddenly the people at the bottom of the stairs were clapping. Campbell, of course, thought it was a party for him. He began to wag his tail, spinning it furiously around and around. He licked my face all over with that big tongue of his, and I knew we were all good again.

He then guided me beautifully through the airport.

After talking with the lady at the reservation counter, I learned that there were no more connecting flights to Charlotte that day that would then connect me to my hometown airport. So I knew I would have to go back to the school.

Suddenly, for whatever reason, I drew a blank and could not remember the number for the school. I was starting to feel really exhausted by then, as well as extremely homesick. I was in tears. I simply could not remember the phone number. Finally, out of frustration and very upset, I called Donnie and asked him for the number. I told him what had happened, and then we were both upset.

I was feeling very confused. On the one hand, I really wanted to go home. I'd even gone so far as to ask the lady at the reservation counter to put me on standby in case someone canceled. But in the end, Jeff ended up coming to pick me up. Although I was upset about not getting to go home, I was so tired and upset by then that I was also quite relieved to be going back to the school for one more night.

When Jeff arrived, we learned about the cancellations of the flights of the three other students who had left the school at the same time I had. So all four of us piled into the small van he'd brought and headed back to the school.

On the way back, I told them what I'd learned about my hometown, about the storms and deaths in the area. Jeff told us there had been a tornado sighted about 20 minutes from the airport, and that was why they'd canceled our flights.

When we returned to the school, everything was very confusing for me. For some reason, they put us in different rooms than we'd been in before. It made me feel even more homesick, because nothing on that wing felt familiar to me. I was also confused about being back there because I'd just gotten used to the idea that I was going home and leaving the safety of the school. Now I was going to have to go through that all over again the next day. On top of that, Drew was not there, of course. Although I'd known that he wouldn't be, it only made me feel more homesick and alone.

When I had Campbell settled on his bed, I went to lie down, and although I had not meant to, I began to cry. I reached for my cell phone and tried to call Donnie at work. The volunteer on duty told me he'd already gone. I called his house; no answer. Then I called his cell, but he didn't answer that, either.

Something didn't feel right. I was starting to get really upset, and the sense of dread that had nagged at me earlier was back, stronger than ever. For just a moment and purely out of habit, the thought went through my head: Well, I'll just go talk to Drew; he can always make me feel better about things. Then I remembered again that he was gone. That made me feel even more alone, and I couldn't seem to stop my tears from falling.

As I lay there crying quietly, I felt a familiar presence in the room. I began to feel sleepy, and as my eyes began to close, I felt as if there were a comforting hand on my shoulder. Campbell sighed contentedly and stretched himself. I gave into the comfort that now seemed to surround me and immediately fell asleep.

I've never spoken to anyone about that brief moment. I'm

not sure what was happening. No doubt many of you are sitting there thinking, Well, you were tired, or your imagination was working overtime. I don't know, but I was glad for it nonetheless. I have learned in these last few years that sometimes the Universe simply provides what we need when we need it.

***

Jeff woke me sometime later to tell me he'd gotten our supper and that I should come to the common lounge to eat.

"Wow!" he said. "You two were sure doing some snoozing. I came by your room to check on you a little while ago, and both of you were really out."

I didn't say anything to him or anyone else about my experience just before falling asleep. I didn't know then, and I still don't know, exactly what to say about it. I just look on it as a gift from someone, somewhere, who knew what I needed when I needed it, and I was thankful.

Once we were all gathered in the lounge, Jeff passed out our food. We'd each ordered some kind of fast food. The food at the school was absolutely fantastic. That's no exaggeration; they served us some of the best food I'd ever eaten in my life. But somehow we were all ready for hamburgers, Mexican, or something else other than good, healthy food.

As we sat around the big table eating, we swapped stories of what had happened to us at the airport. Each of us had had some sort of unusual experience. I asked Jeff what he thought the dogs thought about it all. He laughed and said, "Oh, I imagine they think that was the strangest training trip ever!" We all laughed and settled in for an evening of visiting. Campbell lay happily at my feet.

For a while, I was content just to be there, to feel safe and sure of myself again. As we talked, the CEO himself, Jim Kutsch, came up from the dining room and brought us a couple of trays of cheese, fruit, and crackers, along with a bottle of wine. They'd had some sort of event in the dining room, and they hadn't used everything up. I was happy to have a glass of wine, but remembering my earlier lesson with drinking and the morning after, I had only one glass. It was just enough to take the edge off.

Soon it was time to park the dogs and head to our rooms. We all had early flights the next day. The weather had cleared, and it looked as though we would not have any trouble at all going home.

I went to my room and called Donnie. He actually seemed a bit disappointed that I'd not been able to come home. But he didn't really answer me when I asked where he'd been earlier in the day. Nor did he seem to want to talk very long. So, feeling tired and kind of depressed, I took Campbell and went to bed.

It was all I could do to keep from putting him in the bed with me, but I'd gotten in trouble for that once. I remembered what Drew had said to me when I'd countered his disapproval with my usual sass-mouthed response. "You know I'm going to let him in bed with me when I get home, right?"

He had replied without hesitation. "Yes, young lady, you probably will, and that's your right. But while you're here, I hope that you'll have enough respect for the school and its rules to obey them, and enough sense to know that there will be consequences if you don't. We have reasons for the rules, one of which is that it's very hard to get the dog hair out of the bedspread. But even if our rules don't make sense to you, don't you think it's rather disrespectful to simply have such disregard for the ways in which we do things?"

I had not forgotten that rebuke.

Thinking about it, I figured that no one would know whether Campbell slept on the bed with me that night. I could wash the spread, and with him being on it only one time, I could probably get all the hair out. But I just couldn't do it. I knew that if I purposely did something I'd been told in no uncertain terms not to do, it would be the same as spitting in their faces.

There were a couple of female students in class who thought that Drew was too hard on me. One of them actually went and complained to her instructor about that very thing. When I was asked about it, I laughed. I told them I couldn't be happier with the instruction Drew was giving me. As far as I was concerned, if he was hard on me, it was only when I deserved it. Furthermore, I knew it was a darned good thing that he had the gumption to do it.

As I settled into bed, I was plagued with mixed emotions. On the one hand, it felt comforting to be there one more night, and on the other, I really wanted to go home and see Donnie and my other pets. I missed Celine Kitty terribly, and Rocky and Kitty Bob, too. It seemed like forever since I'd seen them. I was starting to get a little excited about the morning. Still, there was that nagging feeling that something wasn't quite right.

Then, as quickly as that negative feeling had come, strong and pulsing in my head, it was replaced by the same sense of comfort that had filled me earlier. Once again, there was the feeling of a comforting hand on my shoulder.

Sleep finally overtook me, and soon night was slipping away, into the early dawn of a new day.

Chapter 16

Finally Going Home

The next morning came more quickly than I had thought it would. Once again, I got up. Once again, I dressed and made a last-minute check of my room for any forgotten items. I didn't have my luggage, only my backpack. My luggage was waiting for me in Charlotte. It had gone ahead later, but with no connecting flight, it was sitting in a baggage hold someplace waiting for me to claim it.

Once again, we four new grads met in the common lounge for breakfast. Finally it was time to go. Jeff himself was taking me to the airport. He came into the lounge and called to me from the door, telling me he'd already gotten my backpack and had taken it to the van, and that it was time for me to go.

I got up and got Campbell ready. We followed Jeff to the stairs, and I'm proud to say I went down them with no hesitation. Jeff cheerfully congratulated me on a job well done. As I mentioned earlier, there had been two real sticking points for me in training. One had been my problem with confusing left and right, and the other had been coming down from the tops of stairs. Jeff and I were both proud to see that at least one of the two problems was subsiding a bit.

When I commented that I hoped I would also lose the trouble with my sense of direction, Jeff encouraged me by saying, "You'll get better with all of this as time goes on. It's going to become just another way of life for you. You've done a fantastic job, and I know Drew is quite proud of you as his student, as are we all. You did a good job of taking direction and of following instructions. There were a few worrying points, but you've done well at working through them, to the point that we're all completely satisfied with sending you home with Campbell. No one doubts your love for him and your continued devotion and willingness to keep learning and growing with him." He squeezed my shoulder as he walked past.

As we made our way to the van, I hoped that was so. What Drew and the rest of my team thought of me was very important to me, and it still is today.

As you will see if you continue to read, I've made lots of mistakes as a new grad. But I have never made a mistake when it came to continuing to learn and grow with my dog. And folks, if you don't learn another thing from my book, learn this: That's the most important thing in my universe. And the rest of it, my other mistakes? Well, perhaps you can learn from them, and I hope you will. But please remember one thing first and forever: You do not ever know what life might throw at you. I went home with Campbell thinking one thing was going to be. I thought my life was going to be as I had planned it. I was wrong; life had other ideas. And if I had not listened to the voice that continued to speak to me, I'd have been in a real mess.

***

Once at the airport and through security, Jeff saw I was a bit nervous. He asked me if I'd like to step out and catch a smoke before getting on the plane. I said I would, and he asked a security guard if we could go out a side door he saw and let me smoke. The guard said we could, so Jeff coached me out. Once outside, I took a deep breath and lit a cigarette.

I asked Jeff, "Do you really think Drew thinks I'll do all right?"

"Yes," he answered, "without a doubt. He's confident that you'll make a good dog handler and that you'll do right by Campbell. He does wish you had a little more self-confidence, but he's hopeful that will come in time."

I just shrugged, and Jeff said, "That's the very thing he worries about right there. You doubt yourself, and you don't understand why Drew doesn't."

I sighed. "I guess I don't."

"Well, let me explain it this way. All through class, Drew continued to report on how well you took instruction, on how quickly you picked up on things, and on how very much you wanted to do the best you could. He had no doubt that you could handle just about anything. Yes, there were and are a few things that he and the rest of us worry about; there almost always *are* when we send a new handler home—or anyone, for that matter. But Drew is more than sure that you'll know when to ask, should you need help. He also knows that you're a good person and will never allow anything to happen to Campbell. In other words, everyone believes in you but *you*."

I smiled a little. "I'll try to work on that."

As I write this book, I wonder how much anyone really believes in me now.

***

As I finished my smoke and Jeff and I reentered the airport, I heard them calling first board for my flight. Jeff walked me up to the front by the boarding gate, but there was no assistant to meet me. The girl there asked Jeff if he was flying with me. He laughed and said, "It's a beautiful day for a flight to Charlotte, but I'm afraid that I'd have to say no."

The girl seemed very flustered. I was about to suggest that she call and request the walk assist I'd requested when checking in, when a man walked up and asked Jeff what the trouble was. I noticed immediately that Jeff's demeanor changed. He became very professional when he described my problem.

The man turned to me and said, "I'd be happy to escort you myself."

The confusion must have shown on my face, because Jeff quickly explained to me that this was the pilot of the plane—the captain himself, no less. The man introduced himself to me and I shook his hand. I told him it would be Campbell's and my pleasure to be escorted onto the plane by him, and I gratefully took his arm, heeling Campbell politely beside me. We walked easily through the jetway after I gave Jeff a quick hug goodbye. I was excited by this unexpected turn of events, and as I look back on it now, I'm really thankful for it. That's because I had been starting to feel down about leaving the school and returning home, and I had no good explanation for that emotion. Having this nice, unexpected distraction helped to dispel my unease.

Once we were settled in our seat, the plane took off on schedule. Once in the air, when the pilot made his announcements, he added the following to the end of his message: "We have a special passenger on board today. His name is Campbell Lee. He comes from Morristown, New Jersey, and he's a Seeing Eye dog. Let's all please treat him with respect." I felt very proud and a bit embarrassed, but I guessed it was okay.

Campbell couldn't have cared less about any of it. He was curled up at my feet, already wending his way toward Dreamland. I reached down and fondly petted his head. "I love you, Bug," I said, "and I'm real proud of you."

***

The first part of our flight was uneventful. When I reached the Charlotte airport, everything went as scheduled. We had a bit of a wait, so I settled in and made small talk with the others waiting in the area.

I had the pleasure of talking to a very smart little boy about four years old. I talked to him about what kind of dog Campbell was. I asked him, "Do you know what kind of dog this is?"

He was sitting on the floor with Campbell after having very politely asked permission to pet my dog, and he said matter-of-factly, "Why, he's an American dog," as if I were the dumbest person on the planet.

I smiled, and tried very hard not to laugh. "Yes, he is an American dog. That's correct. But do you know what he does?"

Again the little boy answered as if I really ought to know this, "Well, yes, he travels in America."

I explained to him what Campbell's job was, and he listened very intently. When I'd finished, I asked, "So, now, what kind of dog is he?"

The little boy, who was starting to sound just a tad exasperated with me, said, "He's an American Seeing Eye dog."

He was a delight to talk to, and I hope he will remember our conversation. I know I will.

When the mother found that their flight was going to be delayed longer, she excused them, after thanking me for taking the time with her little boy. Then they went off in search of something to eat.

When we boarded the second plane, I was immediately distressed. It was small and cramped, full to capacity, and I had a seatmate. I slid over to the window seat, but soon regretted having done so. Campbell just wouldn't fit the correct way. Finally my seatmate and I changed places; he was supposed to have had the window seat anyhow. It turned out that he was from Texas and was getting ready to study in the canine division of his police department. He had a good understanding of dogs in general and also knew something about guide dogs, because his sister raised pups for another school. He was very kind and understanding, and he kept reassuring me that it was all okay—

that I was not doing anything wrong, and that there was really nothing to do but what I was doing.

At last we were landing, and my seatmate and I were saying goodbye. I thanked him for helping me keep Campbell positioned in such a way that he wasn't too bad a hindrance to the other passengers and for being understanding.

Then Campbell and I were in the terminal, and my dad was there. He'd already collected my luggage. He took my backpack from me as well, after being properly introduced to Campbell. As it turned out, I got to show Dad immediately what Campbell could do. Dad simply couldn't properly sighted guide me and carry all that stuff at the same time, so I followed him out of the airport, across the huge parking lot, and to his car with no problem whatsoever. Once again, I was proud as punch of my dog, and Campbell took it all in stride, wagging his tail all the way. He was happy to have something new to do and somewhere new to go. He was happy to be with me, and I with him.

I knew then that we'd be together forever. I was home at last with my boy. I had made it. It had really happened. I'd graduated from The Seeing Eye's Guide Dog Training Program and brought home this beautiful boy. And I had no idea what lay ahead of me.

Chapter 17

Introducing Campbell to My Life

Finally my dad and I made it to the house. Donnie was in the yard when I got out of the car; he came over and gave me a hug. Campbell, not knowing who Donnie was, immediately walked in between us. My dad chose that moment to take a picture, and we all laughed. But even as happy as I was to be back home and feel a real hug from Donnie, I had something nagging at the back of my mind. I chalked it up to a bad attack of nerves and once again pushed it firmly out of my mind.

This was a new beginning for me. A new chapter of my life was being written right in front of me. Hell! I was writing my own chapter, and I didn't even know it yet.

But right then, I only wanted very much to go upstairs to my apartment, settle in, see my cat, and just be at home. Donnie told me that our friend Bob was visiting, and I was okay with that. Bob, who's in his 80s, was and still is a permanent fixture in our home, a real part of our everyday lives, so I wanted Campbell to get to know him. To me, Bob is like part of the family, so having him there was only natural.

I took Campbell to park, even though we'd stopped along the road and let him park there. He was in a strange place, with many new things to see and smell, and the last thing I wanted right off the bat was an accident in the house. I didn't need guide dog training to teach me that an excited, nervous dog should be totally empty before being taken into a strange place for the first time. After all, I'd raised a Beagle, and those dogs are sometimes hard to housebreak even in a great situation, let alone when nervous or excited, so I knew that Campbell should go.

Once that was taken care of, we went upstairs and inside. I took Campbell through the house, allowing him to see inside each room. When we passed my little office/play room, Campbell looked in and then tugged me, wanting to go in. Just when I was thinking I might take him in there and let him look around, since I spent lots of time in there, Celine Kitty decided to show her truest self. She popped her head just a tiny bit out from under the loveseat and spat at Campbell.

Now, for those of you who do not know anything about cats, let me enlighten you. When they spit at you, you do not stop to say, "Hey, kitty, kitty!" If you're smart, you continue on your way and you do not look back. Campbell, however, had not been taught this—or if he had, he had most inconveniently forgotten it, because he continued to ask to go in and meet the kitty.

I decided that life would be the best teacher and that we might as well get it over with. So in I went. I even gave Campbell some slack on the leash. He did just as I had thought he would and stuck his big, snuffling, sniffing nose right under the edge of the loveseat. And just as I'd expected, Celine Kitty introduced herself. Once again, she spat at him and added a very vicious sounding growl from deep within. Still, Campbell pressed onward, so he was rewarded with a nice smack to the end of his nose. He yelped slightly and jumped back, quickly coming over to me and sitting at my feet. I petted his big head and said, "Well, Bug, I guess you've met Celine!"

I took him on through the house, and when we reached my bedroom, I let him sniff around. We made our way over to his crate. I showed it to him, tapped on it, and said, "Campbell's crate!" in an excited, happy voice. I removed his harness, gave him a long leash, and then inside the crate he went. I unhooked the leash, reached in, and petted him all over, telling him what a great job he'd done and what a good boy he was and all. Then I shut the door and went into the office to see if I could talk Celine into forgiving me.

She meowed a small meow, then came slowly out from under the loveseat and jumped up onto my lap. She had all her claws out and managed to poke me in several unhappy places while settling on my lap. She was clearly saying to me, "You were gone 26 darks and all you brought from the gift store was a huge, hairy, stinking dog? *Really?*"

After I showed her the bag of cat treats, opened them, and hand-fed her several, she began to purr. After only a few minutes, though, Campbell was upset and barking. He was so loud that even from the other room, he sent Celine Kitty hissing and running underneath the loveseat once again. She lived under there for the next week, only coming out at night, after Campbell was tucked snugly in his crate.

My dad helped me get some things unpacked and talked to me while I was feeding Campbell; he also went with me to walk Campbell again. Then he said his goodbyes and left us. Donnie, Bob, and I settled in the living room, and I put Campbell on a tie-out at the end of the couch next to my chair. He immediately hopped up on the end of the couch, curled himself into a puppy ball, and promptly fell asleep.

The three of us sat talking for a while, sharing a smoke, and I answered their questions about Campbell and our time together during training. It was wonderful to see that Donnie was finally showing interest. He kept telling me how pretty Campbell was and what a good dog he seemed to be.

He'd gotten Campbell a treat at the store, a big chew bone, and I'd let Campbell have it earlier. I let Donnie be the one to give it to him. I sat beside them, had Campbell go through a quick round of obedience, and then allowed Donnie to give him the chew bone. What none of us had expected was that Campbell would eat the entire thing within 10 minutes. So we decided rather quickly that we'd have to find a different type of chew bone for that set of jaws. We got a great laugh out of the incident, though, and Campbell got a new nickname out of it, as well. I began to sometimes call him Chain Saw.

Things began to settle down for me, and I began to feel more comfortable. I decided that my earlier bad feelings must have just been fear talking, and that it would be okay. I would soon learn just how wrong I was.

***

As the evening wore on, Donnie and Bob decided to go downstairs. Bob was getting ready to leave, and Donnie said that one of our other friends was going to stop by later for a few minutes. I reminded him that I didn't want a bunch of people upstairs in my apartment. I told him that he could have anyone he wanted in his lower part of the house, but not to expect me to come and hang out right away. He seemed a little put off by this, but said nothing.

When I came down a little later to walk Campbell again, one of our other friends was in the driveway. He called out to me, "Beautiful dog, man!" I called back, "Come and meet him!"

I had Campbell lie down in the grass and let him get petted by this newcomer. Donnie and I had a lot of drop-in company, and I wanted Campbell to become comfortable around a lot of different people, but I didn't want to overload him right at first. This particular friend understood, and after requesting and then taking a couple of pictures to send to his wife over his phone, he left us alone.

Throughout the evening, a few more people stopped by, but I seemed to always be outside with Campbell when we met up with them, and this seemed to be working well. Finally, the evening drew to a close. I was worn out and was pretty sure that Campbell was, too, so we called it a night.

That was when one of our first traditions was born. I went over to his crate with Campbell on his leash, singing, "Go to your crate! Go to your crate!" in a happy, upbeat tune and clapping my hands. Wagging his tail, Campbell ran to the door of the crate; as I opened it, he reached out and put his big mouth around my arm. I removed his leash, tucked him inside, and gave him a kiss. "I love you, Baby Bug; go to sleep." He settled in, and I heard no more from him that night.

Chapter 18

Exploring Our New Life Together

For the next few days, Campbell and I simply relaxed, getting to know each other and our new surroundings together. Although I'd known pretty much all there was to know about navigating the property with my cane, I learned rather quickly that it was somewhat different with a dog. Campbell avoided things I had used as landmarks, so the first thing I had to get used to was walking in a new pattern around the yard. The way Campbell chose to take me when I put him in harness and worked him around the yard and house was different than the one I'd used when walking around with my cane. Bushes, trees, the downspouts on the corners of the house—all those things, of course, Campbell steered me right away from. Once I got used to it, it was a pretty neat thing.

After we'd spent a couple of days resting and getting over training, Donnie taught Campbell and me how to get around the block. First I asked him if he'd watched the DVD they had sent about coaching and such. He said he had. We talked about the process anyway.

Campbell and I had a lot of adjusting to do, but I have to admit that there was a whole lot more than I'd expected. Part of the reason was that Donnie was always trying to correct the way Campbell walked through a parking lot or even down a sidewalk. He didn't understand why we walked to the left. I tried to explain it to him, but he never understood. I tried to explain how walking that way kept us out of a lot of traffic, both vehicular and pedestrian, but it was no use. Finally I gave up and simply tried to do what I knew was right.

I found that sometimes Campbell and I made mistakes, and when I'd sit at home in the evenings, I'd think them over. I would realize that nine times out of ten, it was because of mistakes I'd made letting Campbell follow Donnie, rather than having Donnie coach from behind. I understood one of Donnie's reasons for not doing this. He himself had trouble seeing, and when he walked behind me, he was too far from things in front of us to correctly describe what was coming up. So we tried to compensate by having him walk in front and describe the area as we went through it.

Most times, this worked okay, but on other trips out, it was more of an issue for us. That's because Donnie had more of a vision problem than either of us had previously realized. I now know more about this, things I've learned from other high partials, and I always felt that Donnie would have benefitted from a dog. But I wasn't sure he was cut out for the responsibility of owning and handling one.

Right from the beginning, Donnie felt I spent too much time with Campbell, and he made no secret of that. We argued about it sometimes, but I refused to back down, no matter the consequences. I refused to allow Donnie and our problems to destroy all the work that had gone into this magnificent dog and into me as a student—now a graduate—of The Seeing Eye school. Drew and others on that team, as well as my fellow students and other staff, had helped to shape me; I was and still am today truly grateful for that. I know that if I had not had the guidance of Drew's experience to start me on my way, I would never have made it.

I am certainly not saying that I couldn't have worked with another instructor, that I could not have become a good handler by working with any of the other instructors there. However, I had periods during training when I became stubborn. I always did what Drew asked of me, but I know my attitude changed a lot from day to day due to my bipolar. On top of that, if I felt insecure, I could really turn on the sass mouth. Drew tolerated that for only so long, and when he'd had enough of it, I was always clear on that on the first warning, and seldom had to be given a second.

I know it was a challenge for Drew. He was so very kind and patient with me whenever I felt bad. Sometimes by the end of the day, when I would be extremely tired and in the most amount of pain for the day, I would become easily distracted or forgetful. This caused problems with my sense of direction, my ability, and my confidence, and it was during those times that I could become the most difficult. Drew's way of working with me was fantastic. He knew when I needed him to be tough, and he knew when I was just too tired to go any further. Sometimes he would even make me stop when I really wanted to keep going.

I felt I was very fortunate to have had Drew as my instructor, but when I would talk to Donnie about the things Drew had taught me, although Donnie listened, I knew he wasn't taking the time or trouble to retain what I was saying. I also felt that he didn't take me nearly as seriously as I needed him to. Sometimes he would even say that I must be over-dramatizing my descriptions of training. In fact, he said that a lot.

Another thing we argued about was the fact that even though Campbell was now getting small amounts of freedom off his tie-out at home, I was not ready to turn him loose in Donnie's house. After almost three weeks of Donnie's constant bitching, one evening I stupidly decided to give in and give Campbell a minute or two off tie-out. My mistake was not putting our dog Rocky out in the garage first. Although Campbell and Rocky had gotten along from the very beginning, right down to their having destroyed our plan of how they would meet one another, I still should have separated them at first. I did not, however, and what happened was a true mess.

Campbell and Rocky chased each other around the loveseat for a minute, and then Campbell peed—right where he was, behind the loveseat. I immediately took him outside and gave him a bit of correction. But I wasn't too harsh with him, because I felt guilty; I knew I had set him up to fail.

I never mentioned the peeing incident to anyone, not even when they sent someone down to do my follow-up after we came home. I was ashamed of myself. I'd known better, and I felt that I had let the school down, somehow, for having been so weak about it. It would be some time before I told anyone what had happened.

After walking Campbell, I came back in to see how bad it was. Campbell had peed in the carpet. However, considering that the whole house was carpeted except for the kitchen and the bathroom, he didn't have a lot of choice.

As I came through the door, Donnie yelled at me.

"I thought you said the damn dog was housebroken!"

I stepped back a little; he seemed to be really angry, and something in his voice frightened me very badly. All of a sudden, alarm bells were ringing.

A bit shakily, I said, "Well, he is, but that was too much stimulation. I should have done it differently." I went on to explain about how Campbell should have been allowed about five minutes free with no other animals around, and no more than that.

But Donnie didn't understand. He yelled at me again and said, "I don't know if I want the damn dog back in the house! Hell, Rocky's never had any special training, and he's never peed in the house!"

There were other difficulties as well. Donnie found out that Campbell would jump up and catch French fries. Although I asked Donnie repeatedly not to do that without asking me, and only on very rare occasions, I learned from one of our friends that he was doing things like that when I wasn't looking. One day, I was quite sure that he was giving Campbell food he wasn't supposed to have, and I promptly told him to cut that shit out. I explained in detail, in no uncertain terms, that he was undoing Campbell's training, and that I wouldn't have it.

We had a fight about it, and about halfway through, Donnie yelled, "I think you'd choose that dog over me any day!"

I stood perfectly still, took a deep breath to calm myself enough that my voice would not shake, and then said softly, but very firmly and clearly, "Donnie, don't ever ask me to choose between you and the dog, because you will always come out second."

And that, my friends, was only the beginning of the problems I faced.

If anyone tells you they have never had so much as one problem with a loved one, with a partner, family member, or close friend, they are almost certainly lying to you.

I write of this (and I'll write of other difficult things, as well, and even more openly in my next book), because I want you to realize that if you are going through such things, you're not alone. If the one you're having trouble with really loves and respects you, or if you're friends, and the other person truly respects and cares for your friendship, you'll work it out. If you don't, you probably didn't need that person in your life anyhow. That's harsh, but it's how I feel. No one and nothing will ever come before Campbell, or before any other dog I have after him. I know that very well.

***

At the same time that I was experiencing these bad things, these conflicts with Donnie, I was also doing very positive things whenever possible. They included going back and forth to work on my own, and those trips were fun. Campbell and I had learned to walk safely to the bus stop. At that time, we had to cross three side streets, the first of which had a stop sign. This could be both good and bad, but mostly bad. That is, people don't generally come to a full stop at a stop sign, and so even though this sign gave me the right of way, the area drivers didn't always obey it. So I had to be sure before I crossed that street or any other.

You just never know if a driver actually sees you. That's in spite of the fact that I wear reflective or brightly colored clothing, and Campbell's harness has reflective tape on it. And let's not forget that I'm no lightweight, and neither is my big black dog. So I never understand when a driver honks and then says, "Sorry, I didn't see you!" I want to shout back, "Well, what the hell were you looking at instead?" But I don't. I just go on and hope for the best.

Campbell does a great job, so my morning walks to the bus stop and then home again in the afternoon were a wonderful way for us to build our confidence together.

Once I got to work, I then had to make my way into the building. Just as it had with walking around the property at home, walking into work changed suddenly and completely, now that I was no longer cane traveling. Things I had gotten hung up in with my cane seemed to have disappeared; I simply never perceived them, because Campbell zoomed on past them without a second glance. I began to learn about freedom in a way that I had never thought possible.

It was the coolest thing ever the first time I walked on my own with Campbell from the bus stop and then into work. To get into the building, we have to pass this little area where there's a trash can on one side and a stone column and bench on the other. The sidewalk in between them is a bit narrow, but going through that area with Campbell was so effortless that I didn't even think about it much anymore after the first few days. I was so proud to be doing this, and I wanted to learn more about what we could do.

Here is a funny thing that happened shortly after I got home.

About three or four days after my arrival, I had a call from the school. The voice on the other end of the phone told me I'd forgotten some things in my room and that they'd be sending them to me. I asked what I'd forgotten. The woman told me I'd forgotten a couple of outfits and one other important thing. When I asked what it was, she laughed and said, "Your cane."

I was amazed. I didn't even remember leaving it there. I was happy, too, because during class, Drew had practically had to threaten to take the cane away from me to get me to stop carrying it around the building. I didn't use it at the school—not much, anyway—but he kept telling me that I had to learn to rely on Campbell. He assured me that I'd always have help during training when I needed it, and that I'd always be safe. Thus I had gradually let go of the cane, and now here I was being told that I'd left it behind without a second thought. In my mind, that was the best news I could have received. It made me very proud.

***

As the weeks passed, I began to get back into the swing of things at work, and I was slowly getting used to doing things out and about. Campbell and I would go out to eat with Donnie, or we would go shopping and walking downtown to pay bills. And we were getting good at it, at least for the most part.

However, as the summer progressed, I began to want to do more. With just a bit of help from Donnie, I taught myself and Campbell how to walk to our little corner convenience store. I was very proud of having done that, and I wanted to tell everyone. I even wrote about it on the email lists I belonged to. Some shared my excitement, but there were others whose attitude was that I would soon get used to it, so I should just shut up instead of going on and on about it.

I'm happy to say that I have never stopped being excited about new triumphs, no matter how trivial they may seem to others, and I doubt that I ever will. At least I hope not. I've said it from the beginning: When I stop being amazed by these dogs, when I stop caring about learning new things, it'll be time to hang up the harness for good.

It saddened me, though, to see that as I became more and more functional, Donnie didn't really seem to share my joy. Sometimes when we were going out, he would ask me if I couldn't leave Campbell at home. And sometimes he would say to me when we were hanging out together, "Do you always have to have him with you?"

These things hurt me, but a lot of people told me that it would get better with time. People who had partners said that there was always a bit of jealousy at the beginning, and that it would pass. Nonetheless, I wondered. It seemed to me that Donnie simply did not like the fact that he no longer got to decide when and where I went and how I got there.

Chapter 19

Seeing Summer through New Eyes

As spring turned toward summer, Campbell and I began to do more and more on our own. One of the first places I took him by myself, other than to work, was to PetSmart. Now I'm sure that there are some of you dog handlers, especially those of you who handle aggressively scavenging Labradors, who are saying, "What? Are you nuts? You decided for your first trip out in the public at large to go to one of the hardest places in town to work a dog who seems to believe that he's always starving?"

Well, yes, I did. As I've written before, I really like a challenge. I was also finding that I truly enjoyed testing my own and Campbell's limits. I also found that Campbell's work was at its very best when no one else was accompanying us. I figured that we'd never learn to do really neat and hard stuff if we didn't get out into the big middle of it once in a while. And so off to PetSmart we went.

When it came to making my way from the bus in the big parking lot in front of the store to the door, the driver of the bus was very helpful. I simply asked him to describe for me the layout of the walk from there by the bus to the door. Once he did that, Campbell and I were on our way. Then, once I was in the store, I had no trouble getting help.

The funniest thing about the entire trip was that I didn't have any trouble with Campbell while he was visiting with the other animals. No, sir; while we were checking out the cats, other dogs, birds, and other critters, my Lab was as well behaved as one could want.

However, when we walked into the dog food section so I could get an idea of all their different food choices, my dog turned into a sniffing, pulling, whining, two-year-old brat! I'll bet I corrected him at least half a dozen times. He sniffed. I corrected. He pulled toward a display of dog treats. I corrected harder. He whined to see the little baby at the end of a display filled with dog toys. I thought about killing him, and I wondered why these things hadn't happened in class. But all in all, it was a fine trip, and I've been back many times.

Another thing we did that summer was go to block parties. Campbell, Donnie, his son Little D., and I all got up early one Saturday and walked over to the neighborhood park for a really nice summer block party. One of the local churches was putting it on, and what a spread they had! There was a group grilling hamburgers and hotdogs. There was a cotton candy machine, popcorn, and even fresh watermelon. Campbell got himself a tiny bite of watermelon, and he liked it fine. His work was spot on, and even Donnie remarked that having Campbell along made it easier to navigate crowded places. I was able to walk on my own and help carry things, and I didn't have to be assisted through crowds. I didn't have to have someone always going back and forth, making extra trips, until we were all settled to eat.

I also enjoyed going off along the walking path on my own a couple of times, talking to other partygoers, having a picture made of myself with Campbell, and even getting in line and getting an extra piece of watermelon on my own while Donnie and Little D. went off to play a game or two. If I needed to know where something was, all I had to do was to ask directions, just as anyone else would. Many times, people were surprised to learn that Campbell was a Seeing Eye dog and that I was in fact blind. It was so very neat, unlike any experience I'd ever had before. It was turning out to be a fantastic summer.

***

Another thing that Campbell and I enjoyed doing that summer was going over to the home of my daughter, Polly, and letting the kids get to know him. Later in the year, it would turn out that having Campbell would really help out some there. I got so I went quite often, and I helped when my son-in-law, Nathan, had to be away. Also, it was a learning experience that was a whole lot of fun to have.

Polly had a lot of patience with our mistakes. Unlike so many others, she understood that Campbell and I were still learning. She didn't have the attitude that Donnie and so many others had, which was, "Well, why he doesn't do [whatever]?" She understood that Campbell still had a lot of pup in him, and at times she would remind me of that when I got frustrated. The way she went about it was great, too. She would say in a little voice, speaking for Campbell, "Mom, I'm just a little puppy in a great big dog. Give me time!"—or something like it.

She never criticized, and she didn't put me down. Even though she had her own ways of doing things, if I did something in the house that wasn't quite right, most of the time, she would just take a breath and say, "Thanks for helping, Mom. But next time, instead of putting the pots here, how about putting them down in this cabinet instead, okay?"

She didn't start changing her opinion of me till after baby Jack was born, but we were both in kind of a bad place by then, just in different ways, and the stress was huge. As far as that first summer went, it was great.

My oldest granddaughter, Telucia, really took a liking to Campbell, and she was very good with him. She learned quickly that Campbell needed watching if he was in the living room, even when he was on tie-out, because if there were any small toys within reach, he would chew them. I taught her to tell him, "Campbell! Drop it!" She was really good at that, and she told me, "Granny, one day I'm going to go to that school where you got Campbell and train dogs." Of course she'll probably change her mind a hundred times between now and then. But one never knows, and I'd be the happiest grandmother on the planet if she did.

Campbell could even be helpful with the kids at times. On one such occasion I found out exactly how. Cash, who was two going on three, and a very big boy for his age, had decided to rip down the gate in the doorway between the downstairs and the upstairs and take off for parts unknown. Well, I figured I could holler for him till the cows came home, or I could let Campbell help me out.

Campbell, it turned out, absolutely loved Cash, so I took him and said, "Okay, Bug, let's find Cash!" I put him in his harness, and we went off together in search of Cash. It wasn't long till Cash started giggling and gave himself away. Then Katie was there, and we were all on the floor together, laughing. Campbell's reward? That, of course, was licking Cash's face. To Campbell, he always did taste so very, very yummy. No harm was done, and Katie and I soon had the things that Cash had tossed around in the bathroom more or less back in place. We were back downstairs, as if everything were normal (which, by kid standards, they were), when Polly and Telucia came back from wherever they had been.

Those are some of my happiest memories.

***

There was one dark cloud over that summer, though, and the story below still frightens me when I think about how close a person can come to losing someone very special to them in the blink of an eye. Remember that as you read on.

One afternoon in early June, Donnie, Bob, and I were hanging out with the dogs in the garage. We had it dog-proofed, and we were letting them run around. I still wasn't letting Campbell have free time in Donnie's house, but I was allowing him time off his leash and tie-out with Rocky in the garage, to help work on Campbell's off-leash obedience. I wanted to have that somewhat under control before I started letting him run free in the house for any length of time.

As we were getting ready to bring the dogs in and fix dinner, the phone rang. Donnie said it was Polly, so I picked up the extension to see what was going on.

Her voice was strained as she spoke. "Mom, don't get upset; just listen."

I have always hated it when people start a conversation with, "Don't get upset; just listen." In my experience, nothing good ever comes afterwards, and that proved true that afternoon.

"Paw's had a heart attack!" she said into the phone.

"*What?*" I couldn't believe what I was hearing.

"He called me, and I'm following the ambulance onto his street now."

I thought I was going to be sick. Donnie saw my face and led me to a chair. He had put Campbell on his leash, and now he handed it to me. I held tightly to it and listened to Polly as she explained what had happened. I told her I'd come to the hospital and hung up.

I quickly explained to Bob and Donnie what had happened. Donnie told me to go get ready, that he and Bob would drive me over.

I quickly went upstairs and fed Campbell. I didn't worry that it was a bit early. I didn't know what lay ahead, and I wanted to be prepared. I quickly gathered pick-up bags, a couple of paper towels for cleaning Campbell's feet if need be, and my evening medication dose. I tossed these things into a fanny pack and ran downstairs to the yard, with Campbell already in harness. I quickly parked him and went straight to Bob's van. They were waiting, and I was ready to go.

When we got to the hospital, Donnie walked me into the emergency room and to the desk. I told the lady there who I was, and she called someone from the back to escort me to Dad's room.

I turned to Donnie, and he said, "Call me if you need me to have someone pick you up."

"Aren't you going to stay?"

"No, Little D. and his friends are at home."

"Can't you get his friend's mom to watch them? This is an emergency!"

"Honey, there's nothing I can do here, and I really don't want Little D. at their house."

"Can't you get Greg and Terry to watch him and let him spend the night with his friends another day?"

Again he made an excuse. "Well, who knows what they're doing?"

I gave up and went with the nurse, who was waiting for me. I was scared to death, crying, and couldn't believe that once again, Donnie was not going to be with me when I really needed him. This was the second time in three months that he'd let me down. I remember thinking as I walked away, Thank Goddess I have Campbell! At least I'll never be alone as long as I have him.

I held tightly to Campbell's harness handle, which had the desired effect. Campbell's work was fantastic. He followed the nurse perfectly and paid attention to every detail. When he saw my dad in the bed, he went around and past the nurse to get to his side. Campbell had already taken a great liking to Dad, and he knew immediately that something was wrong. He did not try to go right up to Dad; instead, he stopped me by his bedside. I remember being amazed at how well he was doing. At the same time, I was feeling guilty for being focused on that instead of keeping my mind on what was happening.

Dad's heart attack was still going on, and it was a scary thing to watch. I reached out and took his arm; it was ice cold. He was cold all over and shivering. I was horrified; I hope I never see anything like that again. Dad was in pain and very frightened. He tried to be brave, but you could tell. I thought of at least a thousand things I wanted to say, but all I could manage was, "I love you, Dad."

"I'm all right," he said, and I couldn't help but think that that was the stupidest thing I'd ever heard my father say. I also remember thinking the dumbest thoughts. The one that stands out the most is, Dad, don't you dare die. I don't want that to be the last thing you say. His telling me that he was all right while having a heart attack was simply not right. He was not okay. That was Dad, though, always trying to protect me.

Then they were taking him away to do a procedure, and I was left with Polly and the rest of the family. My uncles were there, and although I was glad to see them, I was having a hard time answering their questions about Campbell. It was their first time seeing him. I was under a lot of stress, and Campbell and I were relatively new together. They were not exactly the greatest of circumstances.

We were finally allowed to go and see Dad. Campbell and I followed Polly in, and Campbell did a good job. As we walked past rows of little rooms with patients in them, I noticed that Campbell was looking into each room for Dad. Again, I was amazed at his work. I heard a couple of people remark about him being in there. One lady said, "Wow! Look at that beautiful Lab!" Another said, "That's a huge dog!" When I got inside Dad's room, Campbell again took me to his side. God love that dog's heart. I never had to ask him; he just did it.

My dad was happy to see us, and I can speak for all of us when I say we were very glad to see him. As we talked quietly, nurses came and went. One asked Dad about Campbell.

Dad tickled me when he answered her. "I was against it at first, but that dog's amazing, and I'm glad she has him." By the time we were ready to leave, he'd talked to several nurses about Campbell, and you'd have thought that my getting him had been his idea from the very beginning. I love Dad, and I was so glad he was there to be that way, to show how much his attitude had changed.

As we were getting ready to leave, I leaned over and kissed Dad's cheek. When I stepped back, Campbell stood up, reached his head up, and gave Dad one big slimy on the side of his face. I almost cried. He only stood up there for a moment, but it was beautiful. Dad has been known to say that the one lick from Campbell gave him a tiny bit of extra strength, and I have no reason not to believe him.

***

After the experience with Dad's heart attack, I began to really think about my life, about how important it was for me to become as independent as I could be. I also began to listen to that nagging little voice in the back of my mind. It was telling me that without a doubt, I needed to know how to work and handle my dog to the absolute best of my ability. The urgency of that nagging had now grown some, and I was not about to continue to ignore it. The realization of how quickly a person can be taken from you had hit home with me. Although I still didn't know all that I thought I knew about what the nagging voice was telling me, I knew enough to get off my tail and start working.

I began to teach Campbell to take the initiative regarding finding his way home when we were a bit off the beaten path. On Sunday mornings, I would walk about two blocks away from the area right around our house, and then I would get out my house keys and rattle them at Campbell, saying, "Okay, Bug, let's go home! Let's go see Rocky!"

Little by little, he began to understand what I meant, and little by little, I would take us farther and farther away—always being sure to watch where I was going, of course, so I could retrace my steps, but giving as much control of the trip to Campbell as was possible. At each street crossing or turn, I would let Campbell make the decision whenever possible. If he was correct, I'd praise the heck out of him and encourage him onward. If I should ever find myself truly lost, I wanted to be able to depend on my dog to get me out of a jam. I knew it could be done. Others had told me stories of their dogs having done such things, so I had decided to pay no attention to those who said my dog's memory was not important and couldn't be trusted.

None of that made any sense to me. I'd asked several trainers about it, and they simply didn't understand why folks had that belief. After all, lost dogs have been known to find their way home again over distances of hundreds or even thousands of miles. So why would anyone believe that an intelligent and well-trained Seeing Eye dog would not be able to find its way back home over a distance of a few blocks or miles? That's just nonsense.

One Sunday, when I had taken Campbell several blocks farther away from the house than before, I was thrilled when he worked out the trip on his own and we ended up in the driveway of the house before I had realized we were almost there. I had known it would work, and it had.

Campbell was proud of himself, too. As we went down the driveway toward the house, I praised and praised him. We got inside and cooled off. We had our water, a big wrestling match, and a love fest, and I shared a banana with him. Then he fell asleep, happily curled up at my feet.

Donnie didn't understand the bond we were forming. I believe now that he was a bit jealous of it, maybe even a lot jealous of it, but that was okay with me. Nothing, either then or since, has ever been more important to me than that bond, and it has served me well.

Many things changed for me that summer. Some were wonderful, and I'm ever so happy about them. Others were horrible, and in the end, they would be horrifyingly life changing for me. But all in all, what happened to me that summer made it incomparable, different from any other I've ever had. The only other summer that will ever come close to being as life changing for me was the summer that Donnie, Little D., Old Man Bob, and I went to Myrtle Beach. But that's a story for another day and another book.

As that first summer with Campbell began to really take hold and various changes began to take place, I realized that I was experiencing things that would forever shape me. I was thrilled beyond belief at what was happening to me. It also seemed to me that more and more, Donnie was accepting Campbell, and that renewed my hope.

Chapter 20

Changing Seasons, Changing Lives

As summer got into full swing, Campbell and I began to really enjoy ourselves together. I learned a lot about him during those long, wonderful summer days, and he in turn taught me a lot about myself. I learned that I could handle things much better than I had thought I could. I also learned that I didn't need to always ask someone else before I went someplace or did something.

One of the most fun things that Campbell and I did that summer was to attend the Volunteer Appreciation picnic. It was connected with work, a Contact-Concern event. Donnie escorted us, and I had the absolute time of my life. It was just wonderful to me that I could walk alongside Donnie or follow behind him through the crowds of people, picnic tables, and chairs. It made me glad to be able to walk among the volunteers and board members, to be able to mix and mingle just as anyone else would. Quite simply, having Campbell had changed my life in ways I had never anticipated.

It was also nice when Donnie and I wanted to walk away from the crowded picnic shelter and catch a bit of time alone and a smoke. I was able to walk hand-in-hand with him and heel my dog.

This was something we hadn't done a whole lot of when I was cane traveling. That's because I didn't have good enough reaction time in situations where I needed to step behind

Donnie or stop holding onto him altogether and use my cane. With Campbell, I only had to change the position of my left hand and pick up the harness handle if I needed to travel unaided at any time. So Donnie and I were seeing a whole new side of what Campbell could do for our personal lives, too.

However, I believe that by the end of the evening, Donnie was a bit tired of hearing how wonderful it was that Campbell allowed me to do so much on my own. I understood that to a certain degree. It had to be difficult for him to realize that I could have gone to the event without him. It had to be hard watching someone that you'd helped regain their independence gain even more, to realize that their need for you was changing.

The thing was, I wanted Donnie to understand that I was with him because I wanted to be, not because I needed to be. I wanted him to stop being such a caretaker and more of a partner. He was having a hard time with that, though, and whenever I tried to talk with him about it, he did not respond well. That night, however, we didn't argue about it. When we got home, he even complimented me on how well Campbell and I had done together that day. I was glad to hear that from him, but it hurt me to hear what I was starting to hear in his voice, and that was distance. It seemed that no matter how hard I tried, something was just not right between us, and I couldn't figure it out.

***

As summer progressed, I began to walk more in the evenings. After supper was over, I would volunteer to walk to the corner store for smokes, sodas, beer, or whatever else we might need for the evening. I always loved to take Campbell on that particular walk, because it was a confidence-builder for us. Once we crossed the two streets we needed to, we were on a long stretch of unbroken sidewalk, and it was fantastic to let

Campbell wind up and go. He would stretch himself out and walk full tilt, really boogie down that long sidewalk. Even when other dogs would come to the ends of their chains or to their fences, Campbell would just ignore them. He would simply blow by them, sniffing and snorting, as if to say, "HUMPH! Not only am I not on a chain or behind a fence, but I'm runnin' with my mom. And when we get to the store, I get to actually go in there!" It has always been obvious to me that Campbell knows darned well that he's special. He knows he's different from other dogs. Furthermore, he's doggone proud of that. And well he should be!

On one such evening walk, Campbell and I got ourselves totally lost. I was walking to the store as usual, Donnie was home cleaning up after dinner, and I was looking forward to a nice evening of watching TV and playing with the dogs. Donnie seemed to be in a great mood for a change, and the house was free of kids and Donnie's buddies. It would be just us.

Campbell and I were almost to the store, when suddenly he stopped right in the middle of the sidewalk and would not move. I encouraged him forward, but he would not go. I encouraged him to find a way around whatever was in the way, but he would not do it. I reached forward slowly, to see what had stopped my dog. Although the sidewalk was sometimes blocked by a car or bike, it had no breaks in it and no curbs, nothing that should get this type of reaction from him.

As I reached out, my fingers touched some sort of machine. I felt as far to one side and then the other as I could, and like Campbell, I saw no safe way around it. I couldn't tell what it was, either, and having no idea what it might do if I accidentally touched something I shouldn't, I decided that I would turn around and go back. I knew another way to the store, but I needed to get back a bit toward the house and onto a different street to get there. I expected to have no trouble doing that, and so off we went.

Well, sometimes things just do not go as we think they will. As we started back the way we'd come, I began to drift a little. Daydreaming while walking is something you can do when the trip you're taking with your dog is uneventful, meaning that you'll encounter no steps or street crossings, but you should never simply space out, and that is exactly what I did. Somehow, at the place where we should have turned right, we ended up actually angling out into the street and then crossing to the other side. I realized this was happening way too late. I was already crossing the street. I'd learned that going back from the middle of the street and trying to correct could be dangerous, so instead of retracing my steps, I went ahead and crossed.

Now, what I should've done immediately when I got to the other side was re-cross the street. But no! I decided that I would walk down the street on that side a bit. Not remembering that I was on the other side of Wilcox rather than on Garden, I made a huge mistake. Where I was would not lead me to the other end of Garden, as I expected. It would not put me on the right side of the street to go back and redo the trip in the other direction.

So what ended up happening was that I got myself totally turned around and lost. On top of this, I did not have my house keys with me, and they had always been Campbell's trigger to let him know in no uncertain terms that I wanted to go home. I tried unsuccessfully to say, in an upbeat voice, "Campbell, let's go see Rocky!" I tried to figure out where I should turn myself around, but I only confused myself and Campbell more.

Although I was now completely lost, and I knew that it must be starting to get dark, I was fascinated by being on such unfamiliar ground and by being able to navigate as I was. Even though I didn't know anything about the places I was walking, I did not stumble and stagger, as I would have with a cane. With a cane, had I gotten lost the same way I was at that moment, I'd have simply hunted for a driveway, gone to the house at the end of it, and taken a chance with whoever came to the door.

This, however, was something of an adventure, and for a bit, I literally forgot about being lost. Campbell seemed to be as turned on by having something new to do as I was by the realization that yes, I might be lost, but I was still managing to keep my feet under me and my wits about me.

Like Dorothy, I was soon reminded very forcefully that we "weren't in Kansas anymore." That was when we began to go down a long street, and I realized that the street to my right had to be one of our main streets in town. That's because there was suddenly a huge amount of traffic. It still amazes me that twice, I tried to flag down a car, and twice, it seemed that they sped up rather than stopping to see what on earth a blind girl and her dog were doing out at night, alone on a busy street.

I'm still not sure, but I kind of think we had started toward another store that Campbell, Donnie, and I walked to sometimes. I remember laughing to myself and thinking, "Damn dog's decided that if he can't take me to one store, he'll take me to another!"

Even with the frustration of being lost, and even though Campbell and I were starting to tire a bit, I still did not panic. When I got us turned around, going back in the other direction, I began to recognize a few things along our way. Suddenly, up ahead of us, I heard voices, and at that same moment, Campbell sped up.

We soon came to the source of the voices. There was a family out in their yard talking. It appeared that they were leaving. I stopped and asked, "Excuse me, can you please tell me the name of this street?"

The lady whom I'd heard talking turned around, and when she saw me, she recognized me. It turned out that she worked for the vet I took Campbell and my other animals to. I remember thinking what a small world it is! They told me where I was, and I explained what had happened. As it turned out, I was actually headed in the right direction. Had I kept going, I would have ended up back on my street—that is, if I'd known where to turn when I reached the other corner. But Campbell and I had been out for over an hour, and we were both quite tired.

When they offered us a ride home, I took them up on it, since I knew the one lady. Finally, we were back in our driveway, and I could not have been gladder to be home. I went into Donnie's house and yelled for him. I didn't really expect to find him there. I knew he would be out hunting for me by then, and I was hoping against hope that he hadn't yet called the police.

I picked up the house phone and called his cell. When he answered, I could hear the absolute relief in his voice. He told me he'd gone to the store first and had seen the machine in the way. Thinking maybe I'd found a way around it with Campbell's help or that I'd gone the other way and doubled back around, he had checked to see. Once he'd been to the store and had found out that I hadn't been there, he had gotten worried. He said he had tried to figure out where we might have gotten lost, but he had been just about ready to call the police when I'd called.

He came back to the house and gave me a huge hug when he got there.

Then he said, "You're going to kill me, you know?"

"Why?" I asked.

"Because I have a surprise for you."

"And why would I kill you for that?"

He handed me a little box. I opened it, and what do you think was inside? It was the cell phone I'd sent for not a week or so before. I'd ordered one of those free phones with so many free minutes a month, and it had come in the mail. Donnie had meant to give it to me when I got back from the store, because he'd forgotten it before.

Oh, how I laughed! I couldn't be angry. All I could do was hug him and laugh. I laughed until I nearly cried.

He asked, "What on earth is so funny?"

I wiped my eyes and said, "Well, here I was out there, wandering here, there, and everywhere, and here you were out looking everyplace you could think of. Meanwhile, here's this stupid, useless phone, lying on this table, doing no good at all!"

Then I went on to say, "But if I'd had that phone, I'd have called you when I reached that machine on the sidewalk, and I would never have had my adventure with Campbell!"

Eventually we settled down, but I was so tired that I snuggled up on the couch and fell asleep. Campbell was absolutely worn out, too, and he fell asleep on the floor beside the recliner I usually sat in.

Later that night, Donnie walked us upstairs. As he left me at the door, he said, "I'm very glad you had Campbell with you. That little adventure you had might not have turned out so well if you hadn't."

I wanted to hold onto that forever. That was the number one thing I had wanted him to realize ever since I had come back from The Seeing Eye, and he finally had. You cannot imagine how happy that made me. I had renewed hope that maybe, just maybe, we could get past Donnie's thinking I didn't need him anymore, and he could learn to be my partner, not my caretaker.

***

As summer continued, I began to really want to walk to work. Donnie and I did it together, but I wanted to learn how to do it for myself. The sticking point for me was this one red light. We just couldn't see our way clear for me to safely cross there, and Donnie said he didn't feel comfortable trying to teach me. I had worked with my local mobility instructor on some things once before, and had not had a fantastic experience with him at that time. I don't really think it was anything he did wrong or that I did wrong. I think I was just so new when he and I worked together that I didn't know how to correctly communicate what I needed from him.

Still not being sure, I wanted to see if The Seeing Eye would have a look. I contacted them and they sent the instructor who had done my follow-up to see me. He worked through the route with me, and he did find a way to do it, but it was so long that I didn't think it was something I would ever work up to doing, and I felt extremely frustrated when we were done. Donnie and I talked it over again, and for a while, it looked as though I simply would not be able to do it.

But as time went along, I wanted it more and more. So I wrote to the training department and asked to have Drew call me. I explained my trouble and waited to see what would happen. I really didn't expect to hear from him nearly as soon as I did.

One morning, as I was coming back inside from parking Campbell before leaving for work, the phone began to ring. I had the screen door open and could hear the caller ID from the bottom of the steps. It was the school's number. I quickly ran up and inside, grabbing the phone before it could stop ringing.

I answered, and heard, "Hello, Ms. Fletcher. It's Drew Gibbon, from The Seeing Eye!"

I tried to catch my breath, and didn't say hello right away.

"Patty, you there?"

"Yeah, just catching my breath. Been running on the stairs."

"Huh? You're running on stairs? I've reached Ms. Patricia Fletcher?"

I laughed. "You should see where I live."

I needed to hurry and catch my bus, so we got down to the business at hand as I ran around, finishing getting ready for work. I explained what my trouble was. Drew said he'd take a look at the instructor's report, talk with him, and get back to me. That was on a Monday morning in mid-July, and I truly did not expect I'd hear from him again for a while.

As I was leaving for work a few minutes later, I ran into Donnie in the driveway. I told him that Drew had called, and he seemed very surprised. "I really didn't think you'd hear from him," he said.

I gave him a hug. "Doubting Thomas, as usual," I teased, and gave him a kiss. Then Campbell and I were off.

Ever since Donnie and I had moved into the house from the apartments where we'd been neighbors for so long and where he had helped to rehabilitate me, I had begun to enjoy a type of life that I had never thought I would. Even the simple act of going to work as an independent person, with no company other than my dog, was a joyous experience. I learned to enjoy freedoms that most others take for granted and never give a second thought. I relish each and every walk, each and every event that I can go to and not have to have so much help that almost everything else is lost to me. I had never known such happiness as I was feeling then, and at that moment, I could not imagine anything taking that away.

Chapter 21

Yes or No?

On the Sunday after Drew called, I was hanging out on the deck when my phone rang. I didn't recognize the number, but I decided to answer anyway. It turned out to be Drew; he was calling from his cell. He had called to get the address of my house and of the building where I work. I gave it to him and listened, fascinated, as he described what he could see on his computer screen. I got tickled at how he pronounced the names of some of the businesses he was looking at. He finally got a bit annoyed with me and said in his best instructor's voice, "All right, young lady!"

But it only served to make me laugh harder. I teased, "Whatcha gonna do 'bout it, Yankee? I'm here and you're there. Huh?"

He laughed at me. "You! Shush!"

He decided he needed a bit more time to look at and think about the area and said he'd get back to me. Just before we hung up, I teased, "Hey, if I go outside and hop up and down, would you see me?"

He laughed. "You silly redneck!"

We hung up. I figured it would be some time before I heard from him again.

***

One evening about midweek, Donnie was upstairs looking for something for me while I was finishing up the supper dishes. By the time he returned, I was done and in my favorite chair. When he came back, he dropped the phone in my lap, saying, "Pick it up and say hello."

"Who is it?"

"Answer it and see," he said in a mysterious way.

I took the phone and said, "Hello?"

Drew laughed. "Strange. He sounds an awful lot like you."

"Well, well, Yankee. How are you?"

Drew and I began to discuss the route. After a while, he talked with Donnie, too, because Donnie understood the things that Drew could see—on his computer screen, I mean—and I didn't. A bit later, Donnie handed me the phone again.

"You know, I could talk to John Keane and see if he'd okay a visit from me," Drew said. John was one of the managers at The Seeing Eye.

That surprised me, to say the least. "You'd do that?" I asked.

"Sure, I'll just tell him you'd prefer to work with me."

"That's really neat. I'd like that."

We talked a bit longer, and as we were discussing a few things, Donnie brought bowls of ice cream in for the two of us. I set mine on the table to let it get a bit softer and kept talking to Drew.

Now, Donnie had heard all my Seeing Eye stories at least twice, and suddenly he said, "Patty! Correct your dog!"

I turned, and reaching out, I saw that Campbell was getting ready to do away with my bowl of ice cream in a single lick. I quickly corrected with a pull to the live ring on his collar and a sharp, "Leave it!"

"What's that dog up to?" asked Drew.

"He's trying to take my ice cream."

Drew laughed. "Ha, ha! Hungry dog! Smart, too!"

I took my bowl in my hands, and at that moment, Kitty Bob,

who hardly ever bothered me about anything, suddenly appeared on the arm of my chair. Before thinking about it, I said, "Get the fuck out of here, cat!"

Drew started laughing harder than ever. "It's a conspiracy!" he laughed.

We chatted a few more minutes and then he said, "Well, I've got to run, so I'll call you in a little while." We hung up.

Donnie and I were both amazed by Drew's offer of help. We knew it was not an everyday thing for one's very own instructor to come and visit.

***

As the weeks passed, I got busy with all sorts of stuff for work, but I also found myself working on little bad habits that Campbell and I had already formed. I didn't want Drew coming down and finding me having turned into a slob about my guide dog work.

One afternoon while I was at work, I decided to take my lunch break outside. Campbell and I sometimes went and walked around out there, talking with people and getting some sun and exercise. It was a nice day and not too warm, so we really enjoyed ourselves, and I ended up spending my entire lunch break outside. When we came back in, filled with fresh air and sun, the volunteer on duty said that someone named Drew Gibbon from The Seeing Eye had called and left a message for me to call back.

I quickly settled Campbell in his place and called him. He told me that John Keane had indeed said it would be okay for him to come visit, and that we should work out when. I told him that since he had made such a wonderful offer, I would leave that up to him and work around whatever he wanted. We finally agreed on October. He said he would call me when he knew what date.

"Drew," I said, "I can't tell you how very much this means to me. I never would have asked this of you. I never expected anything like this. When I wrote, I figured that maybe you'd talk to the instructor who came to see me, look at Google Maps, and then just call me about it." I was near tears.

"It's okay, Patty. You and Campbell are very much worth the trouble. Please don't cry."

I wiped away my tears. "Sorry, you know how I am."

"Yes, I do, and it's okay."

I took a breath to calm myself. "I'll try to make the trip worth your effort," I said. "I never expected you'd come visit us. That's really way above and beyond."

"Well, I couldn't see what it could hurt, and I think it's worth doing. I was happy to offer, and I'm glad to be able to do it."

I hung up, and for just a moment, I sat thinking how very happy this made me. Since coming home, I had thought a few times about what it would be like for Drew to come visit Campbell and me here, but I'd never expected it to happen. It would usually come to me when Campbell and I would do something new and different, or when we would figure something out on our own. At those times I would always think, Wow! Wonder what Drew would say?

Now I also began to think about some of the things that were going on in my private life that I didn't want Drew to know about. I decided that I would need to work very hard to keep those things far away from our visit. I didn't want anything to ruin it.

Donnie was having troubles with his ex. They were serious issues, and we were starting to have very bad personal problems because of them. I did not want Drew finding any of this out. I didn't want him thinking that Campbell was in any kind of danger, nor did I want him to think badly of Donnie. Never before had Donnie been the way he was then. I also believed this mess would clear up. So I didn't want Drew to know anything about it.

***

As July turned to August, I understood all too well why Drew had not wanted to come and work then. Lord, how hot it was that summer! I was very glad we'd decided on October. All the legal trouble had begun that summer, and I hoped that by October, it would be cleared up and things would be back to normal for Donnie and me.

As summer turned to fall, Donnie became more and more distant at times. I thought it was all the legal troubles he was having, so I tried to be as patient as I could. But we fought more than we ever had, and it seemed to me that he was angrier and angrier with me all the time. I got to where I didn't feel comfortable taking Campbell to his part of the house very often. This feeling intensified after a particularly nasty argument between the two of us.

One evening, Donnie and I were really into it. I don't remember now exactly what it was we were arguing about. It was probably money; we fought about that a lot. I felt that we were falling further and further behind in some areas. In my opinion, we needed to tighten our belts some so we could keep our home. Donnie seemed to want more and more to just give it up and move back to the apartments where we had been before. I hated those darned apartments and did not want to go there again.

On this particular night, whatever we were upset about had him super pissed, and he was yelling at me. It really intimidated me when he got like that. My first husband, who was extremely abusive, was like that. I decided I'd had enough and was going home. I was going down the hall, crying, when Donnie suddenly came up behind me, yelling, "Shut the fuck up, you bitch!" and pushed me to the ground.

As I fell, I hit the door facing the living room and hurt my face. I stood up slowly, and as I did, Donnie reached for me. Campbell began to bark furiously. He was on his tie-out, and I have to say I was extremely glad that he was. I had never, ever heard him bark that way, and when I got to him, his fur was raised up all along his neck. I'd never seen that before.

I tried to sooth him. "Mommy's okay, and it's okay," I said gently, petting him, but he had put himself between me and Donnie.

Donnie yelled, "You better shut that fucking dog up!"

I decided not to continue this. I was suddenly frightened of him and of what he might do to Campbell. I quietly unleashed Campbell from the chair, doubled the leash, and started out the door.

Donnie yelled, "That's right. Take him and go!"

I said nothing and left. I quickly took Campbell out to the yard to park. It was getting dark, and I suddenly wanted very badly to be inside my house with the door locked and the bar in place. I did not often do that. Donnie had a key to the sliding glass door, and up to then, I had never needed to fix it so that he couldn't get into my part of the house. But as I started into the yard, I decided that I needed to do so that night.

As I stepped out into the grass, my poor dog began to throw up. He was so upset that he was sick to his stomach. I knelt down beside him, talking softly to him and rubbing his back.

"It's all right, Bug," I said. "Mommy's okay, and Daddy didn't mean it. It's okay."

Campbell was shivering, and at that moment, nothing would have made me happier than to be at least a thousand miles away from Donnie and to never see him again—not because he'd hurt me, but because he'd upset this sweet baby dog so very badly. Campbell was always solid as a rock. Nothing rattled him. We could walk down the street and be right in the middle of a hectic red-light crossing and have five fire trucks go screaming by, and Campbell would never so much as turn his head or miss a step. But seeing Donnie hurt me had rattled him, and that pissed me off.

To me, nothing was then or is now more important than Campbell. No one would hurt him. I was not going to allow anyone to ruin him. Not even Donnie was important enough for me to allow that. Campbell was and is my very best friend. He is my eyes. He is my protector and my keeper of secrets. Just as he did that night, he still holds the key to my very existence.

I took him and went upstairs and into the house. I did lock my door, and I did put the bar in. After calming Campbell a bit more, I put him in his crate. That was his safe zone. I knew he'd fall asleep in there and would be okay. I was still far from calm myself, and I didn't want to have Campbell see me so upset. It would only serve to keep him upset.

After a bit, I heard Donnie on the stairs. I felt sick. He knocked on the door, and not wanting the neighbors to hear any of our troubles, I went to let him in. Before he came in, he asked, "Where's Campbell?" I told him I'd put him in his crate, and he seemed relieved. I assumed that he was asking because he was worried about him. That, however, was not the case. He was relieved because he was afraid the dog would bite him. He had good reason to believe that. When I let Donnie in, Campbell heard him and growled deep in his chest.

I looked at Donnie. "This cannot continue around him. It could ruin him."

Donnie was only concerned with finding out if he'd left any visible marks on me. As I turned to go back to settle Campbell, Donnie reached for me, pulled me to him, and removed my shirt. My heart nearly stopped. My ex-husband used to do things like that, and it usually meant I was about to be beaten for something. I tried to get free of him, but he held me.

"Stop!" he said. "I'm only looking to see if I hurt you." He was trying not to raise his voice, and he was even trying to sound concerned, but the underlying tone frightened me still more.

"I'm all right," I said, "and I'd really like it if you left."

Finally he was gone. After locking the door once again, and after putting the cross bar securely back in place, I sat down in the middle of the living room floor and began to cry.

Suddenly I heard the latches on Campbell's crate snap open, and the next thing I knew, my dog was in my arms. He licked my face. He nuzzled my neck. He laid his head on my shoulder and did all he knew how to do to love and comfort me.

We sat there like that for a long time. I held him and smoothed his fur. I whispered in his ear that I loved him more than anyone in the entire universe, that no one and nothing would ever come between us, and that I would never, ever allow anyone to hurt him. As I sat there with my arms wrapped around him, holding him and rocking him softly back and forth, I said, "Baby Bug, I promise that no one will ever harm you in any way. If they ever try, even the tiniest bit, I will make their lives very, very miserable. You can bet your wigga woo on that." I kissed him and began to feel better.

After a while, I calmed down and got up off the floor. I turned on a little music and went to see how bad the damage to Campbell's crate was. It turned out that the latches were bent but not damaged. I'd obviously not closed them very tightly; otherwise, he would probably not have been able to open them at all. But I was sure of one thing: This dog loved me very much, and it was for damn sure nobody was going to bother me. Campbell had made that perfectly clear.

***

A few days passed, and things began to slowly return to normal. Donnie and Campbell seemed to make up, but things were never quite the same between the two of them after that. That was just one more thing I wanted very, very much to keep from Drew. I had no idea what his reaction to that kind of thing might be. I didn't know if he was the sort of man who would simply figure I'd gotten what I'd deserved or not. Nor did I know if he'd feel that maybe I didn't need Campbell anymore and then try to have him removed from me. I knew it would be very hard for him to make that happen, but I also knew that with his experience, he might be in a position to try.

Drew cared about that dog quite a bit, and I knew it. I knew he was the kind of person who would not sit by and do nothing if he thought for one minute that a dog was going to be hurt, especially a dog from The Seeing Eye. It was very obvious to me how dedicated he was to the guide dogs, and I did not want any kind of trouble from him.

I've thought about that evening a lot over the months since then. I've come to the conclusion that my relationship with Donnie changed forever that day, and there was no way to come back from that. But even with all that, I was still willing to stand by him, to try my very best to help him with what he was going through. Donnie had been very much a part of all that had helped me to regain my freedom, and I very much wanted to help him keep his.

However, I knew that it would soon be time for Drew to come, and I absolutely did not want him knowing about things like what had happened that awful night. Thus I was bound and determined to keep that secret buried deeply beneath what Drew would see. I decided that when he came, he would see a happy, loving couple, one with none of the problems that most any couple has when starting out.

And that would be that.

Chapter 22

Getting Ready and Keeping Secrets

As we moved into August, things began to get busy for me at work. It would soon be time for the United Way to begin its fundraising, and this would mean a lot of extra things for us. My supervisor, Lynn Sorrell, had always taken me to numerous information fairs, where I helped with presentations about our organization and the work we do. Now I knew that Campbell would be with me, and this would only help to increase what I could do for Contact-Concern.

One event that we went to near the end of that summer still stands out in my mind. In fact, it was the source of the picture on the cover of this book. The photo was taken at a picnic given for the Safe House, our Women's Domestic Violence Shelter. We were going to attend the picnic, and I was honored to be among the participants. Combatting domestic violence is very important to me. At this particular picnic, there was to be a ceremony for the victims of domestic violence. We would be standing at the water's edge tossing flowers in. This was done in recognition of these victims, and hence the picture.

It was a very nice picnic, and I was very glad to have been a part of it. I remember standing there at the water's edge and tossing those flowers in, with poor Campbell wanting so much to go into the water and rescue them. I also remember feeling in my heart that he was rescuing me. Yes, every day.

After what had happened at home, I felt a bit like a

hypocrite standing there, but I told myself, "Donnie wouldn't be acting this way if he weren't under so much stress."

Now, I'll bet that at least a thousand of you readers are sitting there right now and wanting to yell at me, "What the hell is wrong with you? How many times have you told victims who call your center not to ever justify what their abusers are doing?" But I couldn't help it, and if you've ever been a victim of such a thing under any circumstances, you understand that. Honestly, it was not until I started to write this book that I truly realized that Donnie was, for whatever reasons, being both emotionally and physically abusive to me.

At any rate, the picnic was a huge success, and I was glad to have been a part of it. It was wonderfully comforting to have Campbell at my side that day.

***

A couple of days after that picnic, I was just snuggling in for an afternoon nap with Campbell and Celine Kitty when the phone rang. I was so nearly asleep that I almost didn't allow myself to listen to the caller ID. But I heard Drew's area code come up, so I had to answer and see what he wanted. I was frightened that he was going to tell me that he couldn't come after all.

"Hello?" I answered.

"Hey there, sleepyhead!" he called out cheerfully into the phone.

"How did you know I was sleeping?"

"Honey, you don't think I had you as a student for nearly a whole month and didn't learn something about how you sound, do you? Why, I've gotten so good at hearing the tone of your voice that I can tell all sorts of things by it."

Suddenly I felt a big knot begin to form in my stomach.

"Patty, you still there?"

"Yeah, sorry. Just waking up."

I hoped he'd buy that. Goodness knows he'd heard me that way enough during class.

"You sure? You sound a bit—I don't know, out of sorts today."

"Yeah, I'm fine, just tired. It's been a busy week. Whatcha mean, wakin' a girl up from her afternoon nap with her daawg, anyhow?" I asked teasingly. I wanted very much to steer the conversation away from me and how I was doing, if possible.

Besides his whistling, Drew had another somewhat annoying habit. He had a way of asking questions that you couldn't lie your way out of. I hated that, because it meant that I could never get by with anything with him.

"Well, I see you still haven't done anything about your education," he teased. I laughed, and that helped to lighten the mood; it took the focus off me a bit.

"Since you asked," he said, "I've called to let you know when I'll be coming. I'll be there on October tenth."

I started the math in my head, wanting to figure out how much time I had to get things situated. It wasn't just my schedule I needed to work on.

"Patty?"

I hadn't even realized he'd asked a question.

"Sorry. Drifted off again."

"Are you sure you're okay?"

"Yes, sir. Sorry. What did you say?"

"I said, are you going to be working while I'm there?"

"No, I'm going to fix it so I can take off the entire time you're here. How long will you be able to stay?"

"Only from the tenth through the twelfth," he answered.

I fell silent again. I'd hoped for a week. Of course I was extremely grateful for what I was getting, and I did not plan to complain, not one tiny bit. But I was disappointed just the same.

"Hey, lady! I'm talking to you! Pay attention!"

He'd turned instructor on me again, and I sat up, trying desperately to clear my head.

"I'm sorry. I've just been really—"

"Yes, I know. You said 'busy.' Now, what's really wrong?"

I sighed. "Well, I don't want to say."

"Why?"

"'Cause it'll make me sound—well, ungrateful."

"You and I have had this talk. The truth is always best."

"Well, this is a complicated route," I said. "I was hoping for a week to practice it after we mapped it out. I'm sorry. I..." I trailed off. I'd been right; that sounded bratty, whiny, and very ungrateful. "I'm sorry, sir. I don't mean to sound that way. You know I'm glad you're coming, even if it's just for a few days."

"I understand. It's okay."

I felt a bit better, but suddenly wondered if I should let him come at all. What if I couldn't keep all this stuff that was going on away from him? What if he realized how I was living, and what if he wanted to take my dog? I knew that was totally paranoid, but I simply could not get it out of my mind.

"Patty, listen. You'll do fine. We'll figure it out. I'll show Donnie what you need to do and the two of you will practice it. I have total faith in you. You'll be walking back and forth to work all the time before Thanksgiving."

I hoped he was right. The school was going to a lot of trouble and expense to send him down, and I did not want to be a disappointment to them or to have Drew's time with me be a waste of money.

We talked a bit more, and I managed to stay on track. He asked me a few questions, and we made a few plans. Then I asked him if we might have time for him to look at one other thing for me while he was here.

"Drew, on the way to a grocery store that I walk to a lot with Donnie, there's a red light that I have trouble with. Think we could look at it?"

"Sure. I'm sure we'll have time for that, too. Stop worrying so much. You've always done that. But it's all okay. Heck, you worry about stuff more than Campbell could ever worry a bone!"

I laughed. "I know; you're right. I'm just—well, I'm a bit nervous about all this."

"Why?"

"Well, I..."

"What?"

"I don't want you to be disappointed in me." I was near tears and wiped angrily at them.

"Honey, I could never be disappointed in you. You're doing a great job. Stop worrying so much. I promise, I'm gonna come down and we're gonna have a great visit. Now talk to me. What's up? What's going on with you?"

"Aw, just work stress. Normal life. No biggie. Like you said, I'm a worry wart."

Drew let it drop, but I had the feeling that this would probably not be the last I heard about it. That's just how he was. He was kind and caring, and you couldn't help but like him. He knew his dogs, too. He had it together where that was concerned, for sure.

After we hung up, I tried hard to fall asleep again. But it seemed that naptime was over, so I decided to get up and get the rest of my day going.

As the weeks flew by, I worked hard to get things at work in place. I wanted that time period to be filled with good, solid volunteers. I wanted to make sure everyone knew I would be off those three days, and that I wouldn't be available unless it was an emergency. I made sure they knew I would check in with the office every day, and of course they could call me if they truly needed me. But I tried to impress on everyone how very important this was to me and to Campbell.

Everyone with whom I work has always been incredibly

supportive of both me and Campbell. I certainly know how very fortunate I am to have this. There are many blind people out there, other guide dog users, who do not have the type of relationship with their coworkers that I have, and I am blessed to have it. I am deeply grateful to all those I work with, both staff and volunteers.

Chapter 23

Arrival Day

As the day of Drew's visit drew closer, I was happy to see that for the time being, at least, things had stabilized a bit more for Donnie and me. We had stopped fighting so much, but I still had trouble getting him to believe that I'd stand by him and that I believed in him—even though it was starting to look more and more as though he would indeed do some prison time.

He was always telling me, "You need to go on and leave me; you need to get on with your life. You'll just end up regretting it if you stay."

I tried and tried to convince him that I loved him, needed him, and did not want to be without him in my life. But he never seemed to believe that I truly believed in him, and that in fact, it was his own attitude, not the attitude of others, that was pushing me away. It was as though he was two different people, and I never knew from day to day which Donnie I would be coming home to.

But right at the moment, for whatever reason, things were better, and I was very grateful for that. I only prayed that it would remain that way while Drew was here. I was concerned that while he was here, the other Donnie, the Donnie I'd not known before, would return, and I was truly worried. The question kept running around in my head: What would I do if that other Donnie did show up? Would I be able to hide that from Drew? What would Drew say if he found out? Would he think what many of the men in my life had, that I deserved that? Would he be angry with me for not leveling with him about what was really going on in my life when I'd requested assistance?

All sorts of crazy thoughts got in my head. At one point, I even thought that if Drew found out what I had allowed Campbell to witness that night, perhaps he would hurt me himself. I knew in my rational mind that that was not a possibility, but the thought was there, haunting me every darned night in my dreams, and I couldn't make it go away.

I remember one night in particular very clearly. I had cried myself to sleep—which, by this time, happened at least four nights a week. I had been thinking about the whole tangled mess when I'd finally drifted off. I dreamed that Drew had learned from someone else, someone I'd trusted with the knowledge, that Donnie had been physically violent in front of Campbell, and he was furious with me. I was trying to get away from Drew and keep Campbell from him. He kept coming at me, saying, "I'm going to have to take him back. You can't keep him if you're going to allow this. You should've behaved yourself. If you had, this wouldn't have happened."

The dream ended as it always did, with Drew grabbing me and pushing me down the stairs of my deck, laughing as I fell, saying, "Serves you right, letting Campbell be around that crap! And pushing you down the stairs is absolutely appropriate, because I know you're afraid of them."

I awoke terrified, shaking all over. I knew this wouldn't happen just as well as I knew my own name, but it was there in my mind just the same. Before now, I have never shared that dream with a living soul, other than Campbell. I never even told my good friend Mike Tate, who was my very biggest supporter through the whole time I dealt with the problems that Donnie and I had.

Once more, right before it was time for him to visit, Drew

and I talked. He called one afternoon to let me know what his flight arrangements were. Again, he noticed that something was not quite right, and again, I had to really work to distract him. Damn, but that man could be relentless! He would get hold of something and he'd ask about it till he was satisfied. I liked that about him, but I had never expected that it could be something I feared.

I'd always loved the fact that he could read me. It had always helped me in my training, and it had helped to make this visit possible, but now it was a worry for me. I was scared to death that something might go wrong. I couldn't bear the thought that he would think badly of me, or maybe even not like me anymore. That was the worst fear of all. I feared more than anything that Drew would see me for what I was becoming due to all this and end up hating me.

I was also starting to really suffer from symptoms of my bipolar, and that was another worry. Drew knew about my bipolar, and he seemed to understand and sympathize, but he'd never seen me in a full-blown episode, and I was terrified that all the stress I was constantly under was going to bring that about before he could come visit and go back. I couldn't stand the thought of his knowing anything about how I could be during something like that.

At least a dozen times, the fear of it nearly caused me to call and cancel, but I knew he would ask even more questions in that case. Also, he seemed to be looking forward to the visit, and if I canceled, he would be disappointed. But somehow, I couldn't let it rest; the anxiety just wouldn't let up.

One afternoon, about a week before Drew was to arrive, I decided I simply had to talk with Donnie about what I feared. I had no idea what a mistake I was making.

Donnie sat me down and assured me that I had nothing to worry about. He said he figured that Drew, given all his work with the public, had seen just about everything. Donnie could not imagine Drew ever turning me away or hating me. His words had the desired effect; they put me at ease, and I dropped my guard. The thing is, I honestly believe that when Donnie said what he did, he really meant it and believed that he was helping me. As I said before, sometimes it felt as though Donnie was two different people. In fact, it felt that way a lot of the time.

***

Finally the big day arrived. Donnie was taking classes for phone customer service work, and I was home alone for the day. I'd stayed up late with him the night before. We'd spent some real quality time together, and I'd worked very hard to give him absolutely everything he wanted and to make certain he was happy and satisfied.

I went over my apartment again. I cleaned and then re-cleaned the counters. I removed everything from the dining room table and put it away, in case we wanted to eat lunch there. I made sure to check the bathroom at least three times before he got there, because Celine Kitty had a few—well, how shall I say?—undesirable habits.

I even went to the trouble of cleaning my room. I made sure everything was picked up and put away in the extra closet in there, and I even made my bed. At the school, Drew had gotten on me several times about leaving stuff lying around for Campbell to get into. Even though he was not *too* bad at it, he did do it some. All I needed was for Campbell to pick this day to find a pair of my dirty underpants and leave them in the middle of the floor in the living room for Drew to find. Even worse, he could come running into the living room with them in his mouth, go flying up to Drew, and drop them in his lap, asking to play tug-of-war. I knew that Drew would never let me live it down if anything like that happened.

Campbell had done such things to me before; but so far, it

was only Donnie he'd done that with. Under no circumstances did I want him doing such a thing with my instructor. If he had, I think I might have had to request a new dog, because the first one might have ended up stuffed and mounted.

***

As I sat on the deck in the sun with Rocky and Campbell, reading and waiting for Drew, I felt both excited and scared. I was starting to have some anxiety, and I felt a bit nervous about how it was making me feel. I was kind of shaky, and I hoped Drew would not notice. But it was only a slim hope, because I knew how observant he could be. He'd shown that many times during training.

Only one time during class had I managed to keep from him the fact that I was sick. Then, one evening during supper, one of the nurses asked me in front of Drew if I was still running a fever. He caught it without missing a beat.

"You didn't tell me you weren't feeling well," he said.

I came back with my usual sass mouth. "Well, I kept up with you in the mall, didn't I?"

"Yes, you did!"

Normally he'd have called me on it. For whatever reason, he didn't, or at least not right then.

Later, though, he caught me coming up from the tech center, stopped me, and said, "You know, I really do need to know when you're sick. It can affect your training, the way you learn and handle things. A lot of things can go wrong if I don't know what's up with you. Honesty is always the best way with me."

That was the talk he had referred to on the phone.

I knew only too well what he would think about my trying to keep all these secrets. However, knowing that didn't serve me well in the end, and there have been many times since that long-ago visit that I've regretted ever keeping anything from him. I think that if he'd known a bit more—maybe not all, but just a bit more—of what I'd been going through, he might have understood a bit better some of what came from me later on.

***

I went and put Rocky back downstairs. I knew it was getting close to time for Drew to arrive, and I also knew that Rocky could sometimes be a bit troublesome with strangers. I also knew that Campbell was going to be beside himself with excitement as soon as he realized who had arrived, so I figured it was just best overall if Rocky met Drew later.

I hated making Rocky go back into the garage, though. I hated that Donnie left him locked in there so much, and we had fought about it often. Whenever I took Rocky upstairs and let him be on the deck with Campbell and me while the gate was up at the top of the stairs, I didn't tell Donnie that I had done so. Whenever I had asked him about it, he had always said no, with no real explanation. But I knew that Rocky loved and needed that time with us.

I also didn't tell Donnie about how I was starting to teach Rocky and Campbell to walk together on leashes. Donnie always maintained that Rocky was hard to handle, but it was not Rocky who had the problem.

However, whenever I said anything to Donnie about how he handled Rocky, he would come back with something like, "You think you're some kind of fucking expert now, don't you? Went up there and got yourself educated and became a dog training expert, huh?"

Sometimes it made me mad enough to want to just haul off and smack the shit out of him. However, given the way Donnie had become, I knew that if I did anything like that, I'd live to regret it. So I tried very hard to restrain the urge. So far, I had been successful.

After I'd put Rocky up and had gone through the house one more time, making sure to check the bathroom once again, I went back outside to wait. I looked at the notes I'd written about Drew's arrival time, and I figured he was on the ground by now. I'd told him which way to come from the airport, but I was worried he would take the wrong exit and end up someplace he had no clue how to get out of. I worried that if he went the wrong way, he'd end up in Limestone or some other out-of-the-way place, and I'd be two days trying to get him out. That might sound like an exaggeration, and maybe it is. But there are places around here where you can go for miles and miles, and it's all woods and country roads. I had no idea what kind of experience Drew had with that sort of thing.

I didn't think about the fact that he had a Droid phone with GPS on it. Nor did I think about the fact that part of what this man did for a living was traveling. My nerves were working overtime, and all I knew was that he should have landed, and he had said he would call.

Finally I couldn't stand it anymore and tried to call him, but got no answer. The phone went straight to voice mail. For one horrible minute I got it in my mind that he might not show.

"Maybe he's changed his mind, Bug!" I said out loud.

Just then, I heard a car drive slowly by. I thought maybe that was him. I walked over to the gate and stood at the top of the stairs, holding my breath. I waited a minute and heard the car coming back. A moment later, Drew was turning into the driveway. I felt a flood of relief and slowly let my breath out. It was all I could do to keep from opening the gate and running down the stairs to greet him. But I thought that might be over the top, so I stood where I was. Campbell had gotten bored with waiting and had crashed on the couch. Of course he had no idea whom or what I was waiting for.

The car door slammed shut. As Drew walked up the stairs

to the gate, I heard him say something to himself about my having been so afraid of stairs, yet here I was living at the top of at least a dozen. I halfway laughed, but still stood where I was.

As he reached in and unlatched the gate, I stepped a bit closer, and when he walked onto the deck, we were a few feet apart. Campbell had still not shown himself, but as soon as Drew spoke, he came to the door. The amazing thing? He didn't run to him; instead, he came to me and waited for me to give permission for him to go. I hadn't expected that at all. I hadn't put him on a leash, as some had advised. I was very proud of Campbell's off-leash obedience, and to be quite honest, I wanted to show it off, and I hoped like hell that he'd behave himself with Drew.

After Drew and Campbell had been reunited, Drew asked, "Got a hug for your old instructor?" I went to him, and we hugged a moment. I cannot tell you how wonderful it felt when he hugged me. All my fear melted away, and for that brief moment, I felt safer than I'd felt in at least three months.

***

After we'd all been reunited and I'd shown Drew the house, we sat on the deck, drinking sodas and talking. We took a few minutes just to catch up and enjoy the warm afternoon. Then we got down to business.

I told Drew that I wanted to show him the red light in question and that I could get to it myself. I explained that it was right at the corner by the little store Campbell and I walked to, and that I had taught Campbell how to work that route pretty much all by myself. I explained further that Donnie had taught it to me before I left to go get Campbell, and that when I had come back, he'd worked with Campbell and me a couple of times. However, in the end, I had taken it upon myself to actually sneak off one afternoon and walk there with Campbell. When I returned, Donnie was coming out of the house and saw me coming back up the street, happy as a clam. He asked, "Where have you been?" I was very proud to tell him that we'd been to the store and back all on our own.

Drew asked what Donnie had thought about that.

I said, "Well, he was proud of me, but he kind of got on me for taking off without telling him."

Drew thought a minute and said, "Well, I guess I can understand that."

Soon I had Campbell harnessed up, and we were off. I cannot tell you how proud I was to be leading the way, to be totally in charge of the trip, because Drew didn't know where he was going. In fact, it tickled me quite a lot when we were walking down the long stretch of Garden Drive and I came upon those stupid little round, acorn-like things all over the ground and warned Drew they were coming up, as Campbell led me around them without so much as slowing down.

There's another thing that happened on that trip that will always live vividly in my memory. As we were coming up on the place where we would turn from Garden to Wilcox, Drew's phone picked that moment to make some sort of weird noise.

Drew laughed and asked, "Do you hear that noise?"

I didn't even think about what I was doing or saying. "Turn that shit off!" I said. "I need to hear the traffic coming up!"

It got very quiet, and I signaled Campbell left and went a little way before I realized what I'd done.

I turned around slowly, and as the wind blew my hair into my face, Drew laughed at me and said, "Very good job! Sorry about that. I guess I was not paying very good attention."

I laughed a bit, and brushing my hair back out of my face, I said, "Well, nice to know I'm not the only one who gets sloppy when away from the eye of the Eye."

We both got a good laugh out of it, then. I felt kind of proud that I'd had the gumption to say that to him, more or less by instinct. It truly did mean that I was in charge of the trip.

When we got to the parking lot of the little store, Campbell wanted to turn there, the way we always did. He started angling in that direction, wagging his tail. I hupped him up and encouraged him to go on past the store. He did, but I could tell he was disappointed.

"It's okay, Bug," I said. "We'll go there later. Come on, let's go show Drew this nasty red light."

Once we were at the corner, it didn't take Drew more than a few minutes of looking at the situation to say firmly, "Absolutely not safe! You and Campbell cannot do that." He explained why, giving the same reasons that the other instructor had given. The crosswalk was not clearly marked, there were islands to worry about, and it was quite evident that it would only serve to confuse the dog and make it very dangerous for both of us.

I immediately felt disappointed, and it must have shown on my face. Drew put his hand on my shoulder and turned me around to face him.

"Hey, come on!" he said. "Don't give up. We just got started, here, and I have a plan, remember? I just wanted to see this up close for myself, that's all. Come on, now. Let's get home and figure out our next steps."

That was Drew, always encouraging me and keeping me going, keeping my spirits up while doing so.

When we got back to the house, he wanted to drive around and see about the route. We drove over to my office building. As we were going around the building, I told Drew how wonderful it was when I was first able to navigate that section with the trash can, the stone column, and the bench with Campbell.

As I spoke, he said, "I think I see that."

I smiled to myself a bit, because I could hear just a touch of pride in his voice. It wasn't lost on him why that was a big deal to me. So many others, Donnie included, just didn't understand. Oh, they tried, and most were polite about my enthusiasm. But it was so nice to be talking to someone who actually understood why that small thing had excited me so much.

***

Once back at the house, we found that Donnie had just gotten home. He came over to the car, and I introduced the two of them. Drew asked him if he'd take a ride back over with us, so the two of them could get on the same page about some things. I was glad to see that he was involving Donnie right from the start. Drew was helping the situation a great deal, and he had no idea whatsoever that he was doing so.

As we drove back, Donnie told him about us walking to Food City. He pointed out a rather large crack in the sidewalk and told Drew that I had tripped over it and had fallen down the first time we had walked there.

Drew asked him, "After she went down, how did the dog react the next time you all went that way?"

Donnie told him how careful Campbell had been from then on, treating the crack like a step. I was absolutely thrilled that the two of them were talking, and that Donnie seemed to be okay with all this. I just sat there petting Campbell, not saying a word unless one of them spoke to me.

When we were back at the house, Donnie got out and said to Drew, "Nice to meet you. I guess I'll see you tomorrow evening."

"Aren't you going to be home during the day tomorrow, either?" Drew asked.

Donnie explained about his training, and I was glad when Drew made a bit of small talk with him. As Donnie walked away from the car, he said, "Come on in when you get done."

"Okay," I said. "I have to go up and feed Campbell first, but I'll be along."

After Donnie walked off, Drew asked, "Will you go to dinner

with me tomorrow night?"

I sat for a moment and then said, "Well, I'll have to check with Donnie first."

I could hear the surprise in Drew's voice when he answered me. He tried to hide it, but it was very evident that he had not expected that response from me. Drew was used to the cocky, sass-mouthed "young lady" he'd had in class. He was not used to hearing me say I needed to check with anyone about anything I did. He was used to having to make me settle down and keeping me on task.

If this change in me hadn't been so sad, it would have been funny.

"Okay," he said, "I'll see you early in the morning. Say about 7:30?"

"Sounds good to me."

I got Campbell and myself out of the car. After I'd done so, I leaned back in and said, "Thanks, dude; I mean it."

I reached out my hand to shake his, but he just took it in his and held it for a moment. I thought he was going to ask me something else, but instead, he simply dropped my hand and said, "In the morning, then."

I stepped back from the car, gave him a smile and a thumbs up, and he was gone.

I turned and walked upstairs, fed my dog and cat, then went down for dinner with Donnie.

That night everything went very well, and Donnie and I did not have so much as a cross word. He shared his day with me, and I shared mine with him—leaving out the parts about Rocky being up on the deck with Campbell and me, and of the boys' lesson of leash-walking together.

Finally Campbell and I went home. I knew I'd better get some rest if I intended to keep up with Drew the next day. I knew we did not have a lot of time and figured Drew would work me hard.

Chapter 24

Like Old Times

When I awoke the next morning, I was disappointed to see that it was absolutely pouring rain. I had not realized it was supposed to be that bad. I didn't think even Drew would work that route in this kind of rain.

When he got to the house that morning, I said, "I didn't know it was going to rain like this. I've learned to work using umbrellas, though, and I have two. Want to go ahead anyhow?"

He laughed at me. "There you are again, worrying for nothing. The weather report says this will be gone by lunch. Let's just do some other things this morning."

I sighed and went to get another cup of coffee. "Want anything?" I asked as I poured my cup.

"No, brought a soda left over from breakfast."

"Soda with breakfast? Bad Drew!" I teased.

"So I suppose you think your coffee is healthier?"

"Well, of course! It has milk in it!"

As I settled back in my favorite chair, I said, "I sure wish you could stay the week."

"Well, that might have been possible to arrange if there were another grad in the area for me to visit."

I seized on that. "Phyllis Stevens lives in Johnson City. That's 30 minutes from here."

"Hmm. Wonder why John Keane didn't mention her?"

I got the feeling he was talking more to himself than to me, so I said nothing at first. Then I asked hopefully, "Do you think they'd let you stay longer if they were reminded about her?"

"Very doubtful," he answered. "It's hard and expensive to change flight arrangements, and also, I only made arrangements for my dogs through Wednesday. Peggy's gone to Canada."

"Canada? Why?"

Drew explained to me that she'd gone to meet with someone about some poodles. I wasn't really listening, though, so I don't remember exactly what he said.

"Well, I suppose we could go and see Phyllis," he said then. "Do you think it's too early to call her?"

I laughed. "Good grief, no! She gets up before God!"

He laughed, and I gave Phyllis a call. She gave him her address so he could put it into his GPS, and he told her we'd be there in a while. He said, "I've got something else to do first."

I wondered what and asked as soon as he hung up with her.

"We're going to Walmart. I want to watch you and Campbell together for a bit, and since it's raining, Walmart's a good place to work."

"Good! You can work with me on the little route between the bus stop there and the doors."

"All right, let's go."

Soon we were off. When we got to the store, all the trouble Campbell and I had had before, with his not turning immediately into the door when I suggested "Right, inside," did not exist. Drew laughed at me when I said, "Damned dog! Just like a sick kid. Make a doctor's appointment and get them there, and they don't have so much as a sniffle. Bring an instructor around and all of a sudden, no more trouble."

He was still laughing as we walked through the store. "Oh, hush, Yankee!" I grumbled at him.

We looked around, and of course Drew found himself three CDs and bought them. Then as was our norm when shopping, we went in search of some junk food, preferably chocolate. Both of us loved the stuff; it was one more thing we had in common. We went to the Subway in there, and Drew bought me a huge cookie with M&M's in it.

Just as I took a bite, a little piece fell off the edge of it. Before I could so much as move one finger, my dog, who until that moment had been lying peacefully at my feet, jumped straight up into the air and caught that little piece as neat as a pin, and just as neatly made it disappear. Oh, I did correct him! But I was certainly annoyed.

Drew said absolutely nothing till we got back outside. Then he said kind of teasingly, "Well, we do know where such behavior comes from, don't we?"

I cringed a bit, and Drew must have seen it. Mistaking my cringe for my thinking that I was in some sort of trouble with him, he followed up quickly with, "Very nice to see you've improved your corrections."

I relaxed a bit. I did not want him to know that Donnie had been tossing fries for Campbell to catch in the air, nor did I want him to know that I'd allowed it even once. He would never hear the part about the argument that Donnie and I had over it, because he'd be too busy chewing my ass for ever allowing it in the first place. I knew what kind of undoing of Campbell's training that could cause. I'd once gotten myself into a bit of hot water over a piece of toast, and I didn't want that again—*at all*. There are some experiences that I don't ever want to repeat.

Once we were back in the car, we began our trip up to see Phyllis. When we arrived at the apartments where she lived, Drew asked me if I knew the way.

"I do, but I haven't had Campbell here before."

"Well, then let's see if you remember enough to work him to her door."

I did just that, and a good job of it, too. Once we'd gotten inside and settled, we chatted for a while, and I introduced Campbell to Phyllis, Emmy, and the two cats. It was the first time Phyllis had seen Campbell, and she was amazed at his size. She loved his slimies as much as I did—well, almost. I don't think anyone loves his big tongue like me. In fact, I think that sometimes people are put off by it. But as I say: If you don't want him to lick you, don't get in his face. Campbell is simply big on love.

Phyllis asked Drew if he would go out with her and Emmy and watch them walk. He said he would, and they were soon gone.

Campbell and I stayed in the apartment with the two cats, Simon and Sara. Sara was not really happy about my being there. She made that very clear; when I tried to give her a pat and say hello, she hissed hatefully at me. But Simon was his usual loving, playful self. After he'd said a proper hello to me, he went and introduced himself to Campbell. Oh, Campbell wanted very much to play, but I told him to settle down.

"You're in your working clothes, young man!" I said. "Settle your big black ass down!"

That was what Drew heard me saying as he walked back through the door with Phyllis and Emmy.

"Big guy getting restless?"

"Yes."

We talked for a few more minutes, and then Drew's Inspector Gadget side showed itself. As we talked, Phyllis got out one of her portable ashtrays. When she opened it, Drew said, "Oh! There's a light in it, no? Maybe that's the computer monitor, no? Wait! Is it the TV? No! There really is a light in there! Let me see that!" He hopped up so quickly I thought he'd leave the ground.

I couldn't help but laugh. I'd never met anyone else who liked weird stuff like that as much as Drew did. Not only did he like stuff like that, but he liked things that would make weird noises, too. He was always doing that junk with his phone during class. We'd be sitting around with our dogs, actually behaving, and here he would come and make that darned phone make some new noise he'd discovered. And there the dogs would go, up on their feet, looking around to see what the noise was and if they could play with it—or, in Campbell's case, eat it. It was just another little annoying habit Drew had.

Finally he gave the ashtray back to Phyllis and told me we ought to get going. Just as I was getting ready to get up, I noticed something on Campbell's neck.

"What's this?" I asked.

Drew came to look. After a minute, he said that it was the beginning of a hot spot, and he explained how to treat it. "If you shave the fur around that and clean it well every day with alcohol, you should be able to clear it up."

I thought no more about it, then. After saying our goodbyes to Phyllis and Emmy, we were off and running again.

As we walked outside, Drew commented, "Sun's going to shine soon. I've got one more stop to make, and then we'll have lunch. By then, we ought to have good weather for taking a look at that route."

Once back in the car, I asked, "So where to now?"

"I'm looking for something I need for my motorcycle and want to go to this shop I found."

"Oh! You mean the Harley place?"

"Yeah, I need to see if they have it there. I've looked all over for one."

"Cool! I love motorcycles!" I said. "Let's go! Maybe they'll let me drive one."

"Not if I can help it!" Drew said, laughing.

"Oh, come on! You're in redneck country, boy. We do all sorts of dumb stuff here. It's always preceded by, 'Hey, y'all! Watch *this*!'"

We laughed and laughed. It was like being back in training with him. I was so glad I hadn't canceled, and I was hoping against hope that Drew was satisfied to see that Campbell and I were really doing okay and actually getting it together.

Finally we were through with motorcycles. Drew had found whatever it was he'd been looking for. While we were there, I saw a beautiful bike that was very obviously something Drew would've loved to have.

I said, "Well, why not buy it?"

"I'd have to buy a tent and sleeping bag to go with it," he said.

"Why?"

He laughed. "Because I'd need those to sleep in after my wife tossed me out on my ass."

We laughed some more.

"Hungry?" he asked.

"Yeah, a little."

"Did you have breakfast?"

I hesitated.

"Patty, did you have breakfast?" he repeated.

"No, I didn't."

He sighed. "Young lady! What am I going to do with you? How many times do I need to tell you that you absolutely should not skip breakfast and that you should not be out working your dog that way?"

I sighed. "I didn't really have time."

"Why not?"

"Because I had to tend Rocky after Donnie left, and then get myself ready before you got here."

"Why doesn't Donnie tend his own dog?"

I wanted very much to get out of this conversation, but I could see no way.

"He has to leave very early, and…"

Drew cut me off. "Who takes care of Campbell when *you* have to leave early?"

"I do, of course!"

"Well, then I see no reason why Donnie can't do that for

Rocky."

I sighed. "Drew, Donnie doesn't think like we do about dogs. He doesn't understand the importance of routine and stuff, and talking about it is useless."

"Maybe I should talk to him."

I turned to him. I was starting to get a little upset. "I kind of wish you wouldn't, Drew. He kind of—well, he gets a bit upset about it sometimes."

I sat there chewing my lip, with my hands clasped tightly together in my lap. I knew what kind of trouble could be caused by a comment from Drew to Donnie about his care of dogs, or lack thereof.

A bit of silence stretched between us, and then Drew said, "What would you like to eat?"

We settled on burgers and fries, then sat inside Wendy's and talked while the rain cleared and the sun came out. Drew had dropped the subject of Donnie and his dog care habits, and I was glad. I also hoped he would not find out about Cassie Dog. That was another horrible thing that Donnie and I argued about quite often.

How old was Cassie? We had never been sure. I guessed that she was now about 15 or 16. She was almost completely blind, could no longer get up and down on her own all the time, and Donnie kept her in a damned crate out in the garage much of the time. More times than not, I would go out during the day and find her in a wet bed. Time and time again, I had told Donnie that she needed to be put to sleep. On top of that, she needed grooming in the very worst kind of way, but he wouldn't let me spend the money on it. I'd caught hell for even mentioning any of that, and so had no choice but to let it go.

Once we were finished with lunch, we were back on the road and headed to my house. I told Drew I wanted to go back by there.

He said, "We're going to leave the car there and walk over

to your office and back. I want you to get a good idea of these red lights, and I want to see the two of you work them safely. I want to be more than sure that the two of you will be okay doing this. I'm rather proud of you for wanting to do this with bus stops all over the place."

I turned to him. "Well, I need to be able to get there in case the bus isn't running. And if it's a nice day and Campbell's been cooped up for a long time in the office, it'll be good to be able to allow him to stretch himself and get some work before going home. You know, I didn't go through all that hell of training just to sit around!"

He was smiling when he said, "Considering that this is your first dog, you really are turning into quite the handler, and I'm proud of you."

That made me very happy, and it's still my hope that he still feels that way about me. It's something I hope for a lot.

As we drove toward home, I drifted off to sleep, and the next thing I knew, Drew was waking me.

"Wake up, sleepyhead! We're home."

I stretched a bit.

"Sorry, dude. I didn't mean to drop off like that."

"No problem. I didn't know you had till I asked you a question and you didn't answer."

"Sorry, what did you ask?"

"I asked if you had decided about dinner."

"In fact, I have. We'd…"

He cut me off. "Oh, good! I found this little place online that I want to try."

I interrupted him. I hated to; part of me wanted very much to go to dinner with him, just the two of us. It would have been very nice to sit and just shoot the breeze with him, to talk about all kinds of stuff. I had even imagined that maybe I could tell him some of what was going on, that maybe he wouldn't think I was horrible for staying with Donnie, that maybe he wouldn't think I deserved what Donnie did sometimes out of frustration—and that maybe, just maybe, he might have some good advice for me.

But that was not to be.

"Drew? Donnie and I would like to have you to our home for dinner."

I lied to him, then, for the first time that I can remember, and I have to say that it actually hurt to do so.

"I asked Donnie last night about my going to dinner with you, and he said he wanted to cook for you. He said he'd planned it all along and that it was a surprise for me."

That, friends and neighbors, was an out and out lie. I had not even mentioned to Donnie the possibility of my going to dinner with just Drew. I knew way better than that by then. So what I had done was ask Donnie if we could have Drew for dinner at our house. Donnie had readily agreed to that, and I'd been quite relieved to have a solution.

"I'm sure you don't get a lot of home-cooked meals while you're on the road working," I continued, "and Donnie is a great cook. We'd really like to have you."

Drew seemed very pleased with that, and once again, I felt that I'd dodged a huge bullet. But lying to him made me feel sick. It was the beginning of a lot of lying to a lot of people.

Chapter 25

The Route and Visiting

Once inside the house, I took Campbell out of harness and sat down a moment to catch my breath. I'd parked Campbell before coming upstairs, and I wanted to have a cup of coffee before we started. I'd taken my midday medication when I'd gone to the bathroom to wash my hands at lunch, and even though I'd had a short nap on the way home, I was still a bit sleepy and felt somewhat disoriented. Drew said he wanted me alert for this, because he didn't have as much time with it as he would like, and he wanted to make sure that if I saw any troublesome places, I'd be sure to mention them to him.

Finally we were ready. As we started down the walk, he asked if I thought the GPS would distract me if he had it set to talk. I told him I didn't know if it would or not, and to go ahead and give it a try.

Soon I was following the directions spoken by the GPS, and Drew was describing things to me as needed. I have to say it was working well for me, but I wouldn't ever want to depend on one all the time. I'd be afraid I'd lose my skill for remembering things. I can see how it would be easy to become lazy and let the GPS do all the work. While I think technology has done a lot to help blind people become more independent, I also find that it has done horrible things to some skills we once held very dear.

As we got close to my office building, Campbell and I began to recognize where we were, and we began to take more control of the trip.

"Very nice job, guys," Drew said as we walked up to the door. As we were going up in the elevator, Campbell's tail was wagging a mile a minute. He was banging it on the wall of the elevator, and as usual, I was scratching his back and telling him what a fantastic job he had done.

"He really does seem happy to be here," Drew said.

"Ha! Wait till you see what happens when this door opens!" I said as the buzzer for our floor sounded.

The door opened and Campbell shot forward as I lifted my hand to signal him out. Those things literally happened simultaneously. Drew chuckled to himself as Campbell and I went quick as lightening to the office door, with Campbell wigging and wagging all the way. I punched in the key code for the door and explained the reason for it to Drew as we went through.

"You have to understand that some of our callers aren't—how shall I say—stable, and we sometimes have people pissed at us. We don't want anyone to be able to come inside our office unless we've invited them in, or unless we've given them the code. By the way, if I didn't tell you already, you cannot tell people where this place is. Of course, to make sure you don't, I could just kill you and leave you in the woods," I laughed.

My coworker Dawn was sitting at her desk as we came inside, and she heard the last part of what I said. "Patty, how horrible! You're not supposed to warn people first!" I laughed and introduced Drew to her. Campbell, of course, had to say hello to her. Dawn explained, "He has to lick the lotion off my hands."

I took Drew around to meet everyone and was disappointed to see that Lynn, my supervisor, was not there. I'd really wanted the two of them to meet.

Soon we were in the phone room, and Campbell took me straight to my desk. He sat beside my feet and looked up at me expectantly. I knew what he was waiting for, and I didn't hesitate to get it for him. I opened the bottom drawer of my desk, reached in, and got out a small treat. I made Campbell go through a round of obedience, as was our way, and then gave him his treat.

"I've done this since we first started coming here," I explained to Drew. "Jimmy buys him a box of these every month when he buys snacks for the office. It's pretty much the only time he gets treats like this. I don't keep them at home."

Soon Drew and one of the volunteers were deep in conversation. I was sitting at my desk answering phone calls, handing out information and referrals from memory. I didn't have my computer and just went with it.

As we started for home a few minutes later, Drew said, "That's some memory you've got there, lady!"

"Oh, I didn't think you were paying attention back there."

"Well, I was, and I was impressed. How do you remember all that?"

"It's no different than your being able to spot problems with dogs a mile and a half away. We've all got our talents, I suppose. Mine is phone numbers, and yours is dogs and directions."

I had to laugh at my own next thought. "Drew! I didn't know you were into D&D!"

He laughed and said, "Shush and walk, young lady."

"Aw, Yankee, did I embarrass you?"

***

The trip back home was great, and we even made it home more quickly than we'd gotten to work. Once back upstairs on the deck, I asked, "So, you still gonna stay for dinner?"

"Sure, how could I refuse? I wouldn't do you that way. If you guys want to share your home and a meal with me, I'm all for it.

I think it's nice."

I was glad he felt that way, but still felt horrible for lying to him.

As we sat on the porch swing, talking and waiting for Donnie, Drew asked me why Rocky stayed in the garage so much.

I sighed. "Because that's the way Donnie wants it, not because I like it." I didn't want Drew thinking I agreed with any of Donnie's dog-handling methods. However, I was glad he didn't know what I had to endure when I went against them.

Soon Donnie was there, and he and Drew got into a discussion about the trip to and from my office building and some things Drew had seen along the way. I slipped away to feed Campbell and Celine and to try to calm down a bit. I was glad Drew was staying for dinner, but I was also a nervous wreck about it. I didn't want Drew to mention to Donnie anything about dog-handling habits or the lack thereof. I didn't want there to be any kind of problem. I just wanted Drew to keep thinking what he was thinking, that we were a reasonably happy couple with no more problems than anyone else. I didn't want him to know about any of Donnie's legal troubles or any of our personal ones. I just wanted things to keep going as smoothly as they had been so far.

We decided we needed a few things from the store, so we all piled into the rental car and started off.

On the way, I said, "Wow! I sure would like a beer with dinner."

"Well, we don't have the money for it, and you don't need it, anyhow," Donnie said.

I didn't mention it again.

Once in the store, Drew and I went to look around and work together just a bit more, while Donnie went off by himself to shop.

Once we'd separated, Drew asked, "So you want beer with

dinner, do you?"

"Yeah, but..."

"That's okay, honey; it's my contribution to dinner."

I started to say something, but instead I just said, "Thanks."

I was thinking to myself, What can Donnie do about it, anyhow?

I have to admit there was a little part of me that absolutely loved the fact that Drew was buying beer to go with dinner. I couldn't help it. Donnie had been kind of a jerk about it, and he hadn't needed to be so rude. I hoped Drew had noticed it and that that was the main reason he was doing it.

Once we'd picked out the beer, we made our way back to the front of the store and met up with Donnie.

"I see you got your way," Donnie said when he saw the beer in Drew's hand.

"My contribution to dinner," Drew said matter-of-factly. "She didn't ask."

Donnie said no more about it, and we went through the line and out to the parking lot.

Suddenly I remembered the red light there that gave me absolute fits. I asked if we might take a look at it, and Drew agreed with no hesitation. We worked the light a couple of times, and then Drew told me he didn't like the driveways that ran in and out of the businesses along the way to the store. He explained that people came in and out of those so quickly that he worried that Campbell would not have enough time to react should he need to stop me.

He said, "I really wish you wouldn't walk through there without someone with you."

I have to say that I've had to disobey his wishes on several occasions since then. But sometimes you just have to do what you have to do. I'm always careful, but I can just hear Drew's reaction, should I get creamed by a car going through there one of these days. He's standing over my hospital bed and saying,

"Damn it, young lady, I told you not to do that!"

Soon we were back home and starting dinner.

As the evening got underway, Drew brought me a beer. I sat down in my recliner with Campbell lying at my feet. Rocky was running around, and he took to Drew right away.

I loved it when Donnie told Drew he couldn't get Rocky to sit for more than 30 seconds, and then Drew went over and had Rocky sit. Next, he held up his hand and said, "Rest!" in a soft but firm voice. Donnie said that as Drew stood there, holding up his hand, Rocky sat perfectly still, looking up at him, waiting to see what he'd do next. He didn't move so much as the tip of his tail. Again, there was this little part of me that was enjoying watching Drew have things go his way. I was not ashamed of it—and come to think of it, I'm still not.

Before I knew it, Donnie was telling me that dinner would be ready soon and sending me to the dining room to clear the junk off his table. As I started to work at that, Drew walked over to help. When we were done, Donnie began to bring the food in. Drew got me a second beer, and we all sat down to eat.

Soon we were deep in conversation. Drew was telling Donnie his version of my time in class. Well, I guess most of it matched mine. You know, that's the funny thing about people and their perceptions. We all see things and events just a bit differently. It wasn't that I lied about anything or that Drew did; it was just that each of us had perceived things a little differently from the other.

Soon dinner was over, and we were clearing the dishes and putting them in the sink to soak. As I started to put my hands in the water, Donnie called back over his shoulder as he started toward the living room, "Let those wait; come and visit."

I dried my hands and followed the two of them to the living room, where we sat around talking and watching TV. As we talked, the conversation somehow got back around to training.

Donnie said, "Sometimes I think Patty makes entirely too

much out of what she experienced up there. I mean, it couldn't have been as hard as all that. She just goes on and on about it."

Suddenly Drew was on his feet, and again, there was a part of me that was enjoying this a bit too much. I knew all too well what Drew's having gotten on his feet meant. It meant that he had something to say, and he was going to be heard. I sat back, finishing my second beer, and let Drew talk.

He started by saying, "Well, I will admit that she does have a bit of an imagination, but this time, I seriously doubt that she exaggerated a thing. Training can be quite difficult. We've got everyone up and outside by 5:30. That means that if you sleep till we make the call over the sound system to feed your dogs and bring them to the park area, you might or might not have time to even pee before you do. If you intend to have any time to yourself before that call, you'd best be up earlier. Then things get going from there."

He continued, "Breakfast is at 7:00, and then the day begins. Normally, since Patty has low blood sugar, I had her out by 7:45, so her energy would stay high enough for the morning's work. We would usually not return till about 10:00 or so. Then there was usually some sort of lecture or other activity in the morning. If not, then usually Patty took that time to groom Campbell or do laundry or clean her room, which I was always getting on her about."

He kind of paused. As he paced past me, he reached out and squeezed one of my toes.

He continued, "Then we had lunch, and again, since she has low blood sugar, we would be back out and on our way again by 12:45. Sometimes we would be out until 3:00, and occasionally later. Once my retrain students went home, it was just her and one other student for me, and the two of them worked their asses off for me. So, no sir; I doubt she exaggerated a thing."

Drew started toward the kitchen and asked me if I wanted another beer. I told him yes. Donnie wasn't drinking. Drew asked him if he wanted one. He declined, saying, "No, thanks"—and not much more.

Drew came back and placed the icy cold bottle in my hand. As I took a drink, I asked Drew what time it was. He told me it was a bit after 8:00, and I got up.

"Where are you going?" Donnie asked.

"To park Campbell."

"I think he can wait a little while."

"No, it's his park time; you know how I am about his schedule."

"I think…"

Suddenly I did not care what Donnie thought. It was stupidity in a bottle, I suppose, but I spoke up anyway and said, "You know, Donnie, I just don't care what you think. Campbell is on a schedule, and I happen to want to keep it that way. Drew, don't you think routine and consistency are important to a dog's world?"

"Oh, here we go," Donnie said. "Little dog training expert's gonna talk."

He tried to make it sound as though he was teasing me, but I knew he meant it. At the moment, I didn't care. Maybe it was the beer; maybe it was Drew's being there; maybe, as I said, it was just stupidity. But I was sick of him.

Drew spoke up then. "Yes," he said, "as a matter of fact, I *do* think that routine and consistency are important, and not just for guide dogs." I took that moment to reach for my dog's leash.

I left them and went outside. I was glad for the fresh, cool air, and I walked around in the yard for a few minutes to clear my head. I'd brought my cigarettes with me. Now I took one from the pack and lit it, breathing deeply and letting the smoke out very, very slowly. I walked around till the cigarette was gone, just letting Campbell sniff and snuff around in the yard. When I returned, the conversation had changed to something on TV. I had no idea how the rest of it had gone, and I really didn't care about that, either.

"Everything come out all right out there?" Drew laughed.

"Yes, it sure did."

We talked for a while longer, and then Drew's phone rang. He hit ignore on it, and Donnie told him he could step into the bedroom in the back if he wanted privacy to talk. But Drew said, "It's getting late. I probably ought to get going. Early day tomorrow. I'll be here by 7:30, Patty, so don't stay up late tonight. We still need to go over that drugstore route you wanted me to look at, okay?"

I got up and walked Drew out.

As we stood on the porch, for one crazy moment, I wanted to grab Campbell, run and jump in the car, and beg Drew to take me with him. Suddenly I didn't want to walk back into that house alone. However, I knew I couldn't just go upstairs to my apartment; I had to wash the dishes. But I absolutely wanted to be away from there.

The moment passed as quickly as it had come, but once again, Drew did not miss the look that had obviously crossed my face when the thought of escape had crossed my mind.

"You okay?"

"Yes, just feeling the beer, I suppose."

"Well, if it's going to upset you like that, we won't have you drink any more of it."

I smiled at him. "I'm okay; don't worry."

He wished me goodnight, and then he was gone.

As I stepped back inside, Donnie stepped from behind the curtain. He had been watching us, and hiding to do so.

Before I could speak, he said, "Do you have this out of your system, now?"

"What?" My head was starting to spin from exhaustion and the beer. "Donnie, what are you talking about?"

"Well, all you've done is talk about going to get Campbell and what it was like and all about Drew. So I just want to know if now that he's been here and you've shown yourself off at home to him, do you now have this out of your system?"

He turned and started to the kitchen, and suddenly, I was simply pissed. I stalked in and demanded, "What the fuck is your problem? Drew didn't do a damned thing to cause you to be acting this way, and quite frankly, neither did I, so what the fuck?"

He turned on me then, and for the next few minutes, what happened was quite a blur. I know one thing for sure. If Drew had forgotten something and had come back to the house, he'd have learned all my secrets, and to this day, I don't know what might have happened if he had. I am very glad he did not return that night, because I wouldn't have wanted him to walk in on that. It was a horribly violent argument, and it didn't end very well, either.

Finally I had the kitchen cleaned up and was on my way to my part of the house with Campbell. As usual, Donnie was apologizing and crying, and as usual, I was telling him it was okay, that I understood he was under an awful lot of stress—the whole thing. But there was a part of me that wanted to run upstairs to my place, call Drew's cell, and beg him to come back, to come and get me. I wanted him to know everything, and I wanted him to get me the hell out of there.

In the end, of course, I did not. In the end, I went upstairs and picked out a different sweater for the next day, then settled Campbell and myself into bed for the night.

Chapter 26

The Last Day

When I awoke the next morning, I did not feel nearly as bad physically as I had expected I would, but my psyche was a mess. As I stood in the shower waking up, I felt as sad as I'd ever felt in my life. A part of me wished I could simply wash myself down the drain and disappear. Another part was angry, and still another was just really confused.

As I stood there shampooing my hair, the fragrance of the shampoo only made me feel worse. It was the smell of the beach, or at least what always reminded me of the beach. It was a mix of coconut and fruit. I can't remember what it was called; I just remember that every time I smelled that smell, it made me long for the days when Donnie and I had walked hand-in-hand along the shore, picking up random seashells and playing in the surf. I would never forget those times, and I wondered where they'd gone.

The sound of the bell on Campbell's collar out in the hallway brought me back to reality. I remembered that I was supposed to be hurrying to get ready, because Drew would be there soon. We had one more trip to make before he went back. This only made me feel sadder as I turned off the water, stepped out, and began drying myself. Even the fresh smell of the towel made me sad that morning. Its goodness was such a contrast with the mess I was inside.

How could things have gone so wrong the night before? I

just couldn't figure it out. I had really thought Donnie was enjoying himself. I'd even thought he liked Drew. I was really starting to feel that Donnie was two people; it was as if he'd turned one off and turned the other on the night before. I was starting to believe him when he said he didn't remember doing some of what he had done, and I was honestly starting to wonder what was going on, exactly.

I'd heard of things like this, of people having mental breakdown issues when under extreme stress. I'd also heard of people showing their true colors when they felt they had nothing left to lose. So I truly did not know what I was dealing with.

On top of that, I didn't realize what this was doing to my own mental stability. I was already getting very sick and had no idea that was happening.

I'd honestly hoped to see Donnie that morning before he left, but as I hurried to get dressed, I heard Rocky barking in the garage downstairs and the driver blowing his horn for Donnie in the driveway, so I knew I would not.

"Maybe it's for the best," I said to the empty room. "We'd just argue again, and Goddess knows we've done enough of that."

I finished getting ready and hoped that Drew would not notice anything out of the ordinary about me. I was tired and hadn't slept very well, but I'd be okay for this trip. It was short, so no problem. I just was having a bit of trouble finding the entrance to the parking lot, and I wanted to see if he could help me with a way to indicate to Campbell exactly what I wanted.

After I'd gone down and tended to Rocky and Cassie, I came back up, got in my recliner, and leaned back. I had a little time before Drew was to arrive, and I just wanted to rest. I pulled my Snuggie over me and closed my eyes. The next thing I knew, Drew was knocking on the screen door, saying, "Wake up, sleepyhead; get your shoes on!"

I told him to come in and stood up slowly, then went over and put on my shoes.

He came through the door laughing at me. "You didn't really have to do that. I was just messin' with you."

I smiled, but it was an effort. I felt horrible, and hoped he wouldn't see. But as usual, he never missed a thing and immediately asked, "You okay this morning? Look a bit pale to me."

"Just didn't rest well last night. You know how I get sometimes."

He walked over to the couch and sat down. I started to my chair.

"Why don't you come sit by me a minute?" he asked.

I turned around hesitantly.

"Come on!" he said, patting the seat beside him. I went over and sat down beside him.

"Now, what's up with you? You really don't look well."

I sat for a moment, thinking. I suddenly wanted to tell him absolutely everything, but at that moment, the thought of the horrible dream about him I sometimes had came back to my mind.

"Nothing's going on," I protested. "I'm just coming down with a cold or something. I have a bad habit of burning the candle at both ends. You know that."

"So, stayed up late after I asked you not to, huh?"

"Aw, you know how it is. Got talkin' and messin' around at Donnie's, and the time just got away from me." Drew reached out to brush a piece of lint off my face, and I flinched away from him. I hadn't meant to; it was just a reaction.

"Sorry," he said. I was just gonna get that lint or whatever off your face. Didn't mean to startle you."

"It's all right."

I stood up and started over to the coffee pot. Halfway there, I realized I didn't have my cup and turned back around to get it.

I turned too fast and got dizzy. I staggered a bit and reached out, putting my hand on the back of the loveseat to steady myself.

"Are you sure you're okay, Patty?"

"Yes. Now who's being a worry wart?" I smiled a little again, and again, it was an effort.

I went and got my cup and started back to the coffee pot. My left arm was hurting, and I reached up and rubbed it without realizing what I was doing.

"Something wrong with your arm?"

"Yeah, I ran into the door frame last night and knocked the shit out of it. It'll be good as new in a day or two. You remember how clumsy I can be."

"Can I take a look?"

"Oh, it's okay; stop worrying about it. Let me drink this coffee, and we'll go." I quickly finished my coffee and got Campbell and myself ready to go.

Finally we were on our way, and at least for a while, things were as normal as they'd always been.

When we made it to the drugstore, that dog of mine did the parking lot perfectly except for one spot, and this wasn't really a bad thing. He took me straight to the sidewalk and passed some of what we would normally do.

"That's all right," Drew said, "He anticipated what you were going to do, so he took you the easiest and safest way to get you onto the sidewalk and to the door. Sometimes mistakes can be allowed. That one worked to your advantage."

Once again, I'd learned something. Drew explained a bit more about what he'd meant.

"Campbell knew that you'd want to come to the door, so rather than going all the way down to the end and walking up, he simply took a little short cut and brought you right here. He did it safely, or I'd have stopped you. You did well, too; I saw the look on your face when he made that little change in direction. You felt it and questioned it in your mind, but you went with your dog. Did you do that because I was behind you and you knew I'd stop you if there was a problem, or did you do it because you were following your dog and not even paying attention to me?"

I thought about it for a moment before answering. I wanted to make sure I answered this question truthfully. It would not serve any purpose to not do so. This was a learning experience, one more opportunity to get information and knowledge from this man whose work I admired more than he would ever know, work that I knew had valuable learning in it for me.

"I followed him because I thought he might know something I didn't. I could hear no traffic to warn me of a problem, and I felt I was in no danger."

"That's my girl. Good job!"

We went inside and shopped around a bit. Campbell immediately indicated the coolers to my left.

"What's that about?" Drew asked.

"I taught him to find those 'cause they have sodas in them, and sometimes I want one."

"How can you tell what's what in there?"

"Well, that's kind of a trick, but here's something that helps me along my way."

I took him over and showed him that on each handle was a tiny bottle in the shape of the brand of the bottles inside. There was one for Coke and one for Pepsi. I didn't know what the other one was, but didn't care.

"Once I find these, I'm pretty sure to pick up one that I'll drink. When I get to the counter, if it's not what I want, they'll change it for me."

"How often are you right?"

I laughed. "You won't believe me if I tell you."

"Try me!"

"Fifty percent of the time."

We both laughed then. Drew had been telling me from day

one, "Take a chance, lady; there's a 50 percent chance you'll be right." I cannot tell you how often I think about those words and then do exactly that these days. Sometimes I just don't know, from one day to the next, what's going to happen in my life.

Hell, much of the time of late, I don't know who I'm going to wake up as. I don't mean that I have different personalities; I mean that with my moods the way they are, some days it's just hard to know how I'll be by the end of the day.

As we went along, Drew found a book on the history of Kingsport to read on the plane. Then we got chocolate raspberry candy bars and sodas and went to check out.

On the way back, Drew showed me something that helped me a lot. He showed me where to cross, so that when I got back on my side of the neighborhood, I wouldn't have to hunt for this particular driveway that I needed to find in order to get back to where I needed to be. It was a pain to do that. Drew saw a different way, and I liked it much better. Once again, I'd learned some things during what was to have been a very simple trip, and I had not had the problems I'd anticipated.

As we walked along, as usual, Drew was describing things we were passing. As we walked past a house for sale, he said, "There's a house I could consider buying if I were to move here when I retired. Good location for walking and catching the bus."

"What would you need a bus for?" I asked.

"Well, if I got so I couldn't drive, I'd still want to go places, wouldn't I?"

We walked a bit further along, and he said, "Well, Campbell old boy, I thought I'd just come down here and take you back home with me, but I see now I don't need to do that."

Before I thought, I stopped and turned around. I knew in my mind that Drew was just pulling my chain, but I reacted anyway.

"Yankee, you ever come down here to take my dog, you'd best have an army with you. You come here on your own trying some shit like that, I'll have you taken out in the woods and you'll never be heard from again. When the school calls to ask what happened to you, I'll just say, 'Drew Gibbon? Haven't seen him. Reckon he had a change of plans.'"

We both laughed, and he said, "I'm just messin' with you. That dog's happier, I believe, than I've ever seen him, and you're doing a fine job with him."

Once we were back at the house, Drew had some time to kill, so I took him into my little office to show him some pictures and video clips. He found my computer a bit hard to run, given that he hadn't used it before.

I asked, "Would it be easier for you if I emailed this stuff to you?"

He thought it would and gave me his email address. I noticed immediately that it was not a Seeing Eye address and said, "I don't think you meant to do that. That's your personal address."

"It's fine for you to have it as long as you don't give it to anyone else."

"Okay, I promise not to abuse it. Campbell's honor."

I meant that, and I have regretted many times some mistakes I made thereafter, while in a serious bipolar episode—which, unbelievably, I am just coming out of after all this time. There's nothing to do for that now except hope that maybe something in these pages will help to sooth a very bad hurt to a wonderful friendship.

As the picture from the domestic violence picnic came up, Drew said, "Wow! That's a nice picture! That's nice enough..."

He trailed off, and I never knew what he thought that picture was nice enough for, but I do know that it's on the front of this book you're reading. I also want you to know that when I decided to use that photo, I had no plan to even mention the domestic violence that was happening in my life. In the beginning, this book was to have been nothing more than a book of 20 short stories about funny and strange things that happened to Campbell and me after I returned home with him. But as things began to unfold, I decided to write much differently.

As we sat there, Drew went back to that picture.

"So, were you honoring survivors of domestic violence or victims of it?"

"Well, we're—I mean, they're all victims; it's just that some survive and some don't."

As I've written many times, Drew doesn't miss much.

"You reworded your answer halfway through. What's that about?"

"Well, my first husband was abusive to me."

He paused a moment and said, "I've often wondered how someone can end up in a relationship like that. I know someone who's been in more than one."

Suddenly my blood turned to ice. I felt sick. Did he know something? Had I allowed something to show? As I sat there on the arm of the loveseat beside him, I dug my fingernails deep into the palms of my hands without even realizing I was doing it, until I felt the blood start. I stood up then and rubbed my hands on my jeans.

I walked over, shut down the computer, and said, "Well, dude, I've had a blast. I cannot thank you enough for what you did here."

"I didn't do anything special, just my job." His voice had a note of distance in it, as though he was halfway distracted by something.

"You with me, Gibbon?" I teased.

"Yeah, why?"

"You sounded like you might be halfway paying attention to something else."

"Oh, just thinking about the picture of you and Campbell by the river. Your boss wrote, 'This is a picture of Patty and her

Seeing Eye dog, Campbell.' But he spelled dog 'daawg.'"

We laughed. "He knew I was gonna try to send that to you," I said. "I'd meant to send it to the Grad Services email address, but never got around to it."

"Well, I'm glad to have it."

I've often wondered, when remembering that day, if Drew still has the photo. Given the fact that I was quite a pest to him for a while, I'm betting he has nothing within a 200-mile radius that reminds him of me.

We walked back into the living room, and he started getting ready to go. He went into the bathroom. I knelt down by the loveseat there on the living room floor and buried my face in Campbell's fur. I was exhausted. I was simply worn out from trying to pretend I was okay. The previous night's argument with Donnie had taken something out of me, and I hadn't bounced back yet.

"Young lady!"

He startled me so much that I fell back on my heels, away from Campbell. I looked up. "What the fuck?"

He laughed. "Sorry, but you have a litter box to clean."

I laughed nervously and went back to petting Campbell.

"Did you hear me?" he said.

"Yes, I heard you. Chill out. We're not in class, you're getting ready to leave, lesson's over, and you're not in charge."

He stood there for a minute, and I suddenly thought that maybe I'd made him mad. I turned around to face him and tried to stand. My legs wouldn't lift me. I reached out for the arm of the loveseat, but found his outstretched hand instead. He helped me to my feet.

"Are you sure you're okay?"

I sighed. "I do not remember your ever having been such a worry wart."

"And I don't remember your ever giving me cause to be."

We stood that way for a moment, then I relaxed my hand

and he let it drop.

He sighed and said, "Well, give me a hug. I've got to go."

I reached for him and hugged him tightly to me. Tears filled my eyes. I knew I'd never see him again. He'd talked about coming back and bringing Peggy with him. I'd told him they could use my apartment and I'd bunk downstairs with Donnie. We had even talked about his maybe bringing their dogs. He'd talked about how he'd like to go to Nashville and stuff, and I'd said that maybe by then Donnie and I would be buying the house.

Somehow, though, I felt that Drew would not do those things. Somehow I knew something would not allow that. I knew Donnie did not want me having anything more to do with Drew, and that he'd see to it that I didn't. Now, somehow, I felt I'd never get to own my home, and I loved it so very, very much.

Drew returned my hug. "Now, don't cry." He reached out and gently brushed away my tears. "I'll be back one day, maybe in about a year, and you'll be buying the house by then. You're going to do great things, honey; I just know it."

I followed him outside and stood at the top of the stairs as he walked away. For a brief moment, I wanted very much to call after him—to ask him to wait, let me toss some things in a bag, and then drop me someplace. I was going to tell him, "I'll explain on the way." For a brief moment, I entertained the thought of taking the Safe House's offer of help should I need it. But as quickly as the thought had come, it was gone again.

I couldn't leave; Donnie needed me. It was my fault when he got so upset with me, just like the night before. I'd known he was upset, and I should've just left him alone. But no; I had to go charging after him, confront him, and throw a fit. Girls who throw fits have to deal with their consequences. I'd heard that more than once in my life and from more than one man, so I should have known better.

Drew was saying goodbye once more. I gave him a thumbs-up sign and a smile. Again, it took great effort. Then he was backing out of the driveway and was gone.

The emptiness and silence that followed were almost too much to bear, so I turned away from them and went back into the house. I was tired out and wanted a nap. I was very glad that Drew had come and that we'd gotten to work together. Now he was gone, and I needed to concentrate on getting things between Donnie and me straightened out. I loved him, and I believed he loved me. I knew he was having an awful time with all that he was dealing with, and I knew he would never have hurt me until this crap started.

Oh, he'd always been a bit sarcastic, and at times, he could and did say things to me that were belittling and hurtful. Sometimes—well, most times—he did things like that in front of his friends. But I knew that men did things like that, so I had always just let it go. But he had not been physically violent with me until all his own problems had started. Well, I could remember a couple of arguments over the years that had gotten out of hand. He'd pushed me a couple of times, but he hadn't done anything really bad.

As all this ran around in my head, I worked cleaning the litter box and washing up the few glasses and cups in the sink. Then I parked Campbell, and putting him in bed with me, I settled in for an afternoon nap. Just before I lay down, I set the alarm, so I'd be sure to be awake long before Donnie got home. He'd expect me to have dinner started and things ready for the evening, and I wanted very, very much to please him.

As I drifted off, I could hear the little sounds the house was making all around me. The outside noises seemed to fade, and the house suddenly seemed to be whispering to me. As my mind slipped toward sleep, I could have sworn I heard a soft voice say, "Be careful, young lady; be very careful."

Afterword

It's now July of 2014, and a lot has happened since that October day in 2011, the last time I saw Drew Gibbon.

First of all, Donnie and I are no longer together. He's now in the Tennessee State Correctional System, and although I'm saddened to see such a waste, I fear that may truly be where he belongs. I'll never know for sure, because even though I've given him every chance in the world to talk honestly, openly, and at length with me, he still refuses. So I've decided to go forward with my life without him. The adjustment has been hard, but I'm slowly putting my life back together. Having my Campbell Bug by my side makes it much easier and a whole lot of fun.

The long-ago time of which I've written is still very fresh in my mind. I'll never forget the good time I had visiting with Drew and showing him that I was doing well with Campbell. Of all the things I've screwed up in my life since that time, Campbell is not one of them. I know he's happy, and except for the fact that he's a bit overweight, he's healthy and doing well. He loves his work and has done wonderful things for me. I think the best thing he's done, other than giving me freedom of mobility, has been the way he's shown me that love does still exist.

Here in the Afterword, I want to stress that I didn't write this book merely to talk about how I made mistakes. No way, friends and neighbors! One of the main reasons I wrote it was so that those of you who have never owned and worked a guide dog, but who have perhaps thought about that, can know that even after my 31 years as a cane traveler, getting a guide dog was worth every bit of the time, trouble, and expense the process involved. In fact, it has been the most wonderful single change I've ever made.

Now, I've seen and heard comments from cane travelers who became offended at what they read from guide dog handlers, so I want to say something important to you cane travelers. That is: I respect the wishes and rights of all blind persons everywhere to use whatever mobility tools they feel most comfortable using. I also understand that not everyone is an animal lover. Nor is everyone cut out to be a guide dog owner and handler.

Let's face it, folks; sometimes that can be absolutely exhausting or even embarrassing. When it's zero degrees outside, and there are seven or eight inches of frozen snow packed on the ground, and you have to get up at 5:30 in the morning and take your dog outside to let him or her go to the bathroom, that is no fun. When your dog eats something he or she is not supposed to, and the result is an upset stomach that causes a bowel movement the consistency of chocolate mousse, and the dog decides to have this problem all over your bedroom rug, that is absolutely no fun. When, for no reason you can possibly discern, your dog decides to throw up while you're at work, and you ask your coworker to grab a piece of paper to put under his mouth, and your panicked coworker grabs a report that someone has been working on all day out of the printer and your dog throws up on it, that is not fun at all!

But when you're able to walk through a crowded park filled with kids, adults, and even other animals, keeping up with your friends while carrying a plate of food without needing help from anyone—well, let me tell you that it's one of the most wonderful feelings imaginable. It makes all the rest of it worthwhile. All the training, all the fears I faced, the grueling pace we had to keep, the pain I put up with from my fibromyalgia and the roller coaster emotions I dealt with due to my rapid cycling, even the hurt of the loss of a very important person in my life—what I have right here, right now, in my life and my heart has made it all worthwhile. I'm talking, of course, about Campbell, this amazing, furry, loving, and sometimes slobbery friend who is a fantastic help to me every single day, without fail, in absolutely every part of my life.

Still, in spite of all that Campbell has done for me and how much I need and love him, I know that being a guide dog owner and handler is not for everyone. So I hope that if you're a cane traveler and you've read this book, you're walking away from it understanding what I'm talking about, but not feeling offended at all.

There was a time when I was very proud of my own cane skills, and there was a time when they served me very well. As a cane traveler, I had many wonderful times out with my blind friends, right here in this wonderful city I live in. They were cane travelers, too. We used to go lots of places and do lots of things, and we had tons of fun. But for me, there came a time in my life when I wanted things that a cane simply could not do for me, so I chose to go to The Seeing Eye and learn to be a guide dog owner and handler. I'm proud of all the things I accomplished during my 31 years as a cane traveler, and now I'm looking forward to 31-plus years of successful guide dog ownership.

I know that I have damaged my relationship with The Seeing Eye. At times, I've even been afraid that I managed to mess things up so badly for myself that I will not be allowed back. I can only hope that this book will help repair the damage. I have no way to go back in time and do one single thing about the mistakes I made, to change one thing I did that I now wish I hadn't. I can only try my very best to recover from those mistakes and do a better job, now and in the future, of controlling my illness and my life. Have I become successful at that? Partially, but I still have miles to go before I sleep.

Now, is it possible that I may become very sick again at

some point in my life? Yes, it certainly is. Can I prevent that from happening? Well, I can lessen the possibility to some degree, but at least at the present time, there is no total, permanent cure for what ails me, no absolute guarantee that I will never again fall into the abyss of severe mental illness. Therefore, anyone who is a part of my life on a regular basis is going to take some risk at some point of being touched in some way by my illness.

Back in March of this year, I was talking with my friend Mike Tate about how I don't want to hurt anyone else or myself anymore—and how, at one time, I wanted to simply shut myself off from the rest of the world. He reminded me that if I ever did that, I would be throwing away a lot of hard work by a lot of people. He also reminded me that there are always two sides to every story. That is, no matter how badly I messed up and no matter what the cause, there were things that others could have done and maybe should have done to help me stop doing what I did.

There will be much more about my past problems in my next book, *The Raw Truth: Campbell's Rambles Continued.*

At the end of the day, we can sit and talk endlessly about could haves, should haves, and (maybe) would haves. We can blame ourselves or others, or we can try to avoid doing that. But the fact is, none of us can ever know what might have happened *if...*

So, several months ago, even in the midst of all my doubts, I knew nothing else to do but to go ahead with my plan to get this book out to the world. I hoped that writing about them would help me put the painful memories someplace where they couldn't continue to hurt me or cause me to hurt others. After that, all I could do—all I can do—is try to go on.

On that note, here is a paragraph from my editor, Leonore Dvorkin, about another of her editing clients:

Christine McDonald, a blind single mother who lives near St. Louis, Missouri, is the author of the autobiographical book

Cry Purple. It tells of her 17 years as a street-corner prostitute and crack cocaine addict in Kansas City. In the Afterword of her book, she talks about how hard it is to put the past behind you, to try to move beyond old pain and guilt, to move forward. She sums up her constant effort to do so with these inspiring words: "Every waking minute of every day, I simply keep trying to do the next right thing." Those are words of wisdom that surely all of us can use.

So what were my goals in writing *Campbell's Rambles*?

First, I wanted to show what getting ready for and going through training was like for me—someone who is not only blind, but who also has physical and mental disabilities. I wanted people to know that it can be done. You have to be ready to work your tail off, though. You have to be tough. But if you want it badly enough, you can do it.

Then I wanted to show everyone who reads this book what coming home with my dog was like, how it took time to adjust to the wonderful world of being a guide dog owner and handler.

Finally, I wanted to help anyone who is going to guide dog school to get a dog, whether it's your first time or your fifth, to remember to set physical and emotional boundaries for yourself and all those you're exposed to. That includes staff members, classmates, and people you meet during your daily training trips. Believe me, those boundaries will be an important safety net.

In short, be careful. Protect yourself and all those you care for. Take to heart the advice given in this book. Know that I did not write this book to cause more harm to anyone. Instead, I want to try to prevent harm, especially emotional harm, from coming to anyone else.

I want nothing more than to assist all trainers of guide dogs, all trainers of both dogs and students, and all those who receive this training to do nothing but have the most joy they possibly can as a result of working with guide dogs. They are a wonderful gift, and I am so very thankful to Morris Frank and all those who helped him to start here in America one of the most important trends to ever take hold in the world.

To read more about Morris Frank, who co-founded The Seeing Eye in 1929, Google his name or go here to read the Wikipedia article on him:
http://en.wikipedia.org/wiki/Morris_Frank

Now I leave all of you with these simple words from someone I will never forget or stop caring for.

"Take a chance; there's a 50 percent chance you'll be right."
— Drew Gibbon, Sr., Instructor for The Seeing Eye

Drew, you and everyone else should know that I almost decided not to write this book. But then I had a thought (as I sometimes do) and decided that if there was one shred of truth in what you taught me (and of course there was), then if I didn't write my book, I'd be throwing away what you had taught me. It's not that failing to write my book would have made me any less of a guide dog owner and handler. It's that if I had decided against completing the book, I would have been throwing away the keys you gave me, the keys that would unlock the doors that closed me in and the chains that bound me. I knew I couldn't do that, because not writing the book would be the same as lying about how I feel, and both those things would simply be wrong.

So here I am. Once again, I'm slowly getting up from yet another fall into a puddle. Once again, I'm taking Campbell's harness in my hand. Once again, I'm turning around and saying, "To heck with that shit, Yankee!" And now, as I embark on authorship, I'm walking on down yet another new road.

I have not one clue where the road will take me, but thank God/Goddess, Campbell Lee Bug Fletcher, Drew Gibbon, and The Seeing Eye, I can keep on walking.

"How do you get there? A little bit at a time." — Abraham Hicks, 2014

About the Author

Patty Lyne Fletcher in Her Own Words June 2014

I was born on November 9, 1967 in Kingsport, Tennessee, where I also grew up.

Currently, I live and work in Kingsport, where I am Volunteer Coordinator for CONTACT-CONCERN of Northeast Tennessee, Inc. The mission of Contact-Concern: To provide a comprehensive telephone helpline information and referral service for those in need. Vision: Facilitate community safety and security as a key supplier of information and reassurance to those in need. Website: **www.contactconcern.org**

About my blindness: I was born one and a half months premature. My blindness was caused by my being given too much oxygen in the incubator. I was partially sighted until 1991, at which time I lost my sight due to an infection after cataract surgery and high eye pressure. I used a cane for 31 years before making the change to a guide dog.

I'm a 46-year-old single mother with a beautiful daughter, of whom I am very proud. I have a great son-in-law and four beautiful grandchildren. I own and handle a Black Labrador from The Seeing Eye named Campbell Lee—a.k.a. Bubba Lee or King Campbell, to give just a couple of his nicknames. I also have a 15-year-old cat named Celine Kitty and a tom named Kitty Bob. I have a Boxer mix named Rocky. He and his brother, Bubba Lee, love to play and romp in the late evenings, and they delight in ganging up on me when I am my busiest.

For more details, including how to contact me, please see my website: **www.dvorkin.com/pattyfletcher/**

About Leonore and David Dvorkin

Leonore H. Dvorkin, of Denver, Colorado, edited this book. I love the table analogy that she uses when talking about the work she does on the books by her editing clients. She says that while they design and build the tables, she sands them, puts the finish on them, and then polishes them up. Every step is necessary before the table is ready to be sold.

David Dvorkin, Leonore's husband, did all the technical work required to get the book published. He also designed the cover. I thank both of them for their time, patience, and tireless efforts to make this project a reality. David also set up and maintains my book-related Web page:
www.dvorkin.com/pattyfletcher/

Leonore and David offer a diverse range of editing and publishing services at very reasonable prices. Most of their clients are blind. So, if you have a book manuscript sitting on a shelf or on your computer, and you'd like some help with making your own dream of being a published author come true, please see their Web page about their services:
http://www.dvorkin.com/ebookpubhelp.html

The Dvorkins are also prolific writers, with more than 25 published books to their credit. David writes mainly science fiction and horror; he wrote two of his books with their son, Daniel Dvorkin. Those were the *Star Trek* novel *The Captains' Honor* and the alternate history novel *Dawn Crescent*. To read about the Dvorkins' numerous books, articles, and essays, please visit their websites:

David's website: www.dvorkin.com

Leonore's website: **www.leonoredvorkin.com**

Almost all of their books are available as both e-books and paperbacks on Amazon, Barnes and Noble, and other major online buying sites. Three of the Dvorkins' books are now in audio format. One of those is Leonore's book about her experience with breast cancer. The title is *Another Chance at Life: A Breast Cancer Survivor's Journey.* You can find that on audible.com. It's also available in Spanish, in e-book and print, under the title *Una nueva oportunidad a la vida: El camino de una sobreviviente de cáncer de seno.*

As of July 2014, editing clients of the Dvorkins include

Ralph and Barbara Alterowitz
Robert T. Branco
Ernest Dempsey (a.k.a. Karim Khan)
Patty L. Fletcher
J. Malcolm Garcia
Howard A. Geltman
Christine McDonald
Tony Medeiros
Jalil ("Jay") Mortazavi
Brian K. Nash
Nancy D. Pelletier
Steven P. Roberts
David Zindell

For more details, see David Dvorkin's home page: **www.dvorkin.com**